WHAT ONLY TEACHERS KNOW ABOUT EDUCATION

The Reality of the Classroom

Keen Babbage

Rowman & Littlefield Education
Lanham • New York • Toronto • Plymouth, UK

Published in the United States of America
by Rowman & Littlefield Education
A division of Rowman & Littlefield Publishers, Inc.
A wholly owned subsidiary of
The Rowman & Littlefield Publishing Group, Inc.
4501 Forbes Boulevard, Suite 200, Lanham, Maryland 20706
www.rowmaneducation.com

Estover Road, Plymouth PL6 7PY, United Kingdom

Copyright © 2008 by Keen Babbage

All rights reserved. No part of this publication may be reproduced, stored in a retrieval system, or transmitted in any form or by any means, electronic, mechanical, photocopying, recording, or otherwise, without the prior permission of the publisher.

British Library Cataloguing in Publication Information Available

Library of Congress Cataloging-in-Publication Data
Babbage, Keen J.
  What only teachers know about education : the reality of the classroom / Keen Babbage.
      p.   cm.
  ISBN-13: 978-1-57886-776-9 (cloth : alk. paper)
  ISBN-10: 1-57886-776-2 (cloth : alk. paper)
  ISBN-13: 978-1-57886-777-6 (pbk. : alk. paper)
  ISBN-10: 1-57886-777-0 (pbk. : alk. paper)
  1. School improvement programs—United States. 2. Teachers—United States. I. Title.
  LB2822.82.B33 2008
  371.1—dc22
                                                                    2007046327

∞™ The paper used in this publication meets the minimum requirements of American National Standard for Information Sciences—Permanence of Paper for Printed Library Materials, ANSI/NISO Z39.48-1992.
Manufactured in the United States of America.

Dedicated to Murphy Jones

CONTENTS

Acknowledgments		vii
Introduction		ix
1	The Classroom Reality: Listen to Teachers	1
2	The Issue: I Don't See How You Do That	21
3	The Frustrations of Reform after Reform after Reform	39
4	The Partial Divide	62
5	The Massive Divide	83
6	Today's Reality: Have You Been in a Classroom Recently?	119
7	What Is to Be Done?	151
8	Lessons Learned	168
Epilogue: Be Like Murphy		180
About the Author		183

ACKNOWLEDGMENTS

Thank you to the high school students whom I taught, learned with, and learned from in U.S. history classes during the 2006–2007 school year. Keeping up with you certainly made that the most exhausting and demanding year of my career. However, our many accomplishments made that the most productive, rewarding, meaningful, and fulfilling year of my career.

One very capable and very kind student evaluated our U.S. history class with these precious words: "Through this class and you, I have become the student that I tried to be for so long." I cherish those words, plus those words remind me that the most important part of improving education is between student and teacher.

The saddest day of my career was during the 2006–2007 school year. About 8:40 a.m. on a day in February 2007, an associate principal came to the classroom where my first-period class met. He asked to see me. He stepped into the hall and the words I heard from my colleague absolutely broke my heart. He told me that a ninth-grade student had died. The associate principal was aware that I had known that wonderful, vibrant, smart, and friendly student because I had been the assistant principal at the young student's middle school during the student's sixth-, seventh-, and eighth-grade years. I had taught this student when he was an eighth grader in my economics class. When I was told that Murphy Jones had died, my heart broke, my soul grieved, my body ached, my mind searched for some guidance.

I quickly prayed and then walked back into the classroom. My students deserved to be taught well. My broken heart had to wait. For the next week or two, I cried often. The tears finally stopped, I thought, but the sadness returns occasionally, and then so do the tears. These tears pause; they never end.

You taught me very well, Murphy. Your creativity, your vibrant personality, your dynamic lifestyle, your unique impact on people all touched many lives. This book is dedicated to you, Murphy Jones, because you dedicated so much to everyone you knew and to everything you did. I hope I taught you as much and as well as you taught me.

INTRODUCTION

"Welcome back to school. We hope that you and your families had wonderful summer vacations. The students will return next Monday, so our work this week will be to fully prepare for the new school year. So, teachers, are you ready?"

The principal's question was responded to with a very limited level of applause, a few cheers, and from most people in the faculty audience, silence. The principal was not discouraged, so he continued his appeal.

"Of course you are ready, but just to help you make the final preparations and plans for the start of school, we have organized three days of outstanding professional development. The theme for this year's professional development is designed to emphasize the teacher as an academic coach and as a mentor to students, so the theme is . . ."

At this moment the lights are turned off, the inspiring music is turned up, the video presentation of multimedia magic begins, and the theme for the year appears: "Academic Coaching and Daily Enthusiastic Mentoring Invigorates Classrooms." The first letter of each word in the theme created the acronym ACADEMIC. The principal smiles broadly. Some of the teachers yawn massively. The school's cheerleaders run in to lead the teachers in an energetic round of "Give me an A, C, A, D, E, M, I, C, what have you got? Academic!"

The principal thanks the cheerleaders, the lights are turned on. The music is turned off. The video has ended. The theme for the year has been introduced. "Now it is my pleasure," the principal states, "to introduce our guest speaker who will lead our three days of professional development. I heard Hunter Boyle three years ago at our state's annual conference of school administrators. His schedule was so busy that I had to book him three years ago to be with us now. Hunter taught elementary school for two years, was a middle school principal for six years, was an assistant superintendent for ten years, and then was our state's associate commissioner of education for regulations, policies, laws, and reforms for ten years. He retired five years ago and travels nationally speaking to educators. Please welcome Hunter Boyle."

The teachers were polite with smiles and applause. The teachers also were silently asking themselves questions that should have been discussed months before as part of the planning for the professional development. "What makes this guest speaker's presentation so good for us?" "Isn't this guest speaker just going to give us three days of his one-size-fits-all speeches, handshakes, stories, videos, and other materials? Then he will take our money and go present the same show to another audience." "Did anyone think of asking teachers what we need professional development to provide?" "Academic coaching and daily mentoring are just trendy words. Why are we following another trend of the year? Let's talk about teaching and about students, not about popular trends that are quickly forgotten."

How did this happen? The principal had good intentions. The guest speaker does provide informative and entertaining presentations. The frustration among the teachers who have to passively sit and listen to generic topics for three days is evident and will increase during the second and third days. Mr. Boyle will be paid much money. The principal can tell the school district superintendent that a nationally known speaker provided the professional development. It might look good on paper, but this is not how the classroom reality is addressed or improved.

Please note, the principal was not trying to impose worthless professional development on the faculty. The principal was sincerely impressed with Mr. Boyle's presentation three years ago and concluded, "I've got to find a way for our faculty to hear Mr. Boyle." The principal's

INTRODUCTION

intentions were honorable, but the teachers are not responding to the intentions or to the professional development as the principal had hoped.

What could be done to get better results for the principal, for the faculty, for professional development, and, above all, for students? Listen to teachers. I know what you are thinking, "Well, some teachers just complain all of the time. If we listen to them and then give them all they ask for, it will just cost more money and not produce anything." Listen to teachers anyway. Most teachers I have worked with will genuinely offer sensible, reasonable, valid, well-informed, realistic perspectives and ideas. Listen to teachers because they know the reality in classrooms. Of course, educational leaders, administrators, reformers, lawmakers, policy makers, regulation writers, or decision makers cannot grant every teacher request or implement every teacher recommendation. Of equal importance is that more educational leaders not deny themselves the unique and vital input that teachers can provide.

Imagine that the principal asked teachers for suggestions about professional development programs and topics that would be useful, practical, beneficial, and realistic. No teacher would reply by saying, "Let's have an expensive guest speaker who will talk to us for several days about very general, vague, trendy topics that do not relate specifically or personally to any problem, any opportunity, or any person at our school."

What has convinced me that efforts to improve education must include significant input from teachers? One, career experience. I have worked in schools for twenty-three years and in advertising for three large companies for eight years. Those companies were at their best when they listened closely to employees and to consumers. Two, the managerial and governmental concept of democracy as stated by Dr. Earl Reum, "People support what they help create." Three, reality. Education happens in classrooms. Every effort to improve education relies on effective implementation in classrooms. The teacher is the person who, more than anyone else, impacts what happens or does not happen in classrooms. Four, recent experience. After being a middle school assistant principal for thirteen amazing years, I returned to the adventure of being a high school teacher in the 2006–2007 school year. It was the most fascinating, exhausting, productive, revealing, and meaningful year of my career. I experienced the classroom reality daily, and I learned lessons that can be taught only in the classroom.

The history of education reform is that another reform always emerges to replace that most recent reform. There are many reasons for that continuous cycle, such as promises made by political leaders, trends that move across the nation or world, new demands in the marketplace for workers with updated skills, unwise decisions about the most recent reform, ineffective implementation of reform, or a change of president, governor, superintendent, principal, or interest group agenda, among other reasons. Perhaps educational improvement should be continuous, but it should also be realistic, practical, sensible, directed toward genuine problems, and shaped in part, perhaps in large part, by the people who are most responsible for causing improved learning to happen in classrooms—teachers. This book explores the idea of educational improvements being based on what is learned by listening to teachers.

The qualitative research done for this book is not presented as and was not intended to be the definitive study that can be precisely extrapolated. The research done for this book does provide compelling insight and authentic commentary. The quotations that are included from the research provide the reader with an efficient way of listening to some teachers and with a reminder of why teachers must be heard.

When case studies or other accounts in this book use a name or present a character, the name and the character are fictional; however, the issues and the ideas are very real.

1

THE CLASSROOM REALITY

Listen to Teachers

Time. The first question teachers were asked as part of the qualitative research for this book was "What are the most difficult parts of your job as a teacher?" The most common answer was time. Listen to these thoughts of capable, conscientious, dedicated teachers:

- "Not having enough time to devote to everything."
- "The long hours and the mounds of paperwork."
- "There are so many demands—grading papers, planning lessons, conferences to attend, meetings, paperwork, parent contacts—and little time to do it all."
- "Time—planning, instruction, communication all take time."
- "Not having enough time to teach, difficult parents, and feeling trapped because we have a set program to implement."
- "The lack of time to do the job well. I have 150 students and fifty minutes of planning time each day."
- "A difficult area of my job is the time it takes managing the paperwork/bureaucracy, which includes things like textbook check in/out, documentation of all discipline encounters and parent contacts, going to meetings. This is not exactly difficult to accomplish, but the time lost to instruction and planning is significant."

- "As an English teacher, the most difficult aspect is keeping up with grading. If a class has thirty-one students, it takes me two to three or more hours to get through one set of essays. Multiply this by five classes, and that's many hours of grading."
- "Managing the paperwork and grading."
- "Extraneous paperwork placed upon teachers from higher up."

Time. When presidents, members of congress, governors, state legislators, school board members, state department of education officials, school district officials, or community leaders offer their ideas, plans, schemes, or reforms to improve education, do any of those people offer ideas that would address the need for teachers to have more time to do the work they are ready, willing, and able to do?

Time. The qualitative research done for this book found that the most serious difficulty facing teachers is inadequate time to complete all of the work of classroom instruction with students, all of the planning that precedes classroom instruction, all of the grading of papers that follows classroom instruction, in addition to every other duty, task, chore, meeting, paperwork, and bureaucratic reporting that is mandatory.

It would be easy for a taxpayer, a community leader, an educational administrator, or a political leader to say, "Every worker in every job would like to have more time. I need more time. Teachers have the summer off, plus other holidays. They really have a pretty worker-friendly schedule."

I wondered about that worker-friendly schedule, so during the 2006–2007 school year I measured the hours I worked each week. The number was always in the seventy-two to seventy-five hours per week range. I would arrive at school about 7:00 a.m. and leave on the average at 5:00 p.m. The school day for students is 8:30 a.m.–3:20 p.m. I would do two to three hours of work per night at home Monday–Thursday and twelve to fifteen hours of work at home per weekend. Add these: ten hours per day times five, two and a half hours per night times four, weekends of twelve to fifteen hours, and you get seventy-two to seventy-five hours per week to do the job well.

Prior to the 2006–2007 school year, I had been a middle school assistant principal for thirteen years. That is a very demanding and complex job that included many evening duties of meetings or supervision, which also included some office hours on weekends to get caught up on paperwork. That job required about sixty-five hours per week during the school year. That job also was supported by people who could provide their unique expertise—secretaries, custodians, school counselors, the school social worker, the principal, school district support staff.

To be quite clear, school administrators have very demanding, complex, and challenging jobs. The duties of school administrators increase annually. A principal could have 50, 100, 150 faculty and staff in the school, all of whom report directly to the principal. How many business executives have 50, 100, 150 direct reports? The organizational flowchart of many businesses would show a chain of command that limits the direct reports for the chief executive officers. For that matter, in a school district, how many direct reports does a superintendent have versus how many direct reports does a school principal have?

Time. Teachers who participated in the research for this book mentioned that the lack of time combined with more and more time-consuming demands placed on teachers is the most significant difficulty they face. What actions are being taken to address these time realities that teachers face? If teachers conclude that the most challenging difficulty they face is related to time, yet education reform efforts add more time demands to teachers, what are the likely results? Results could range from heroic efforts to do the impossible to a reluctant decision to change jobs.

What could happen if there could be increased communication between teachers and people who make laws, policies, regulations, and decisions that impact teachers in particular and what happens in classrooms in general? The goal is not to automatically give every teacher total support for every request made or to totally redress every complaint expressed by every teacher. The goal is for teachers and educational leaders to thoroughly listen to each other and to collaboratively work toward common goals within the overall area of improving student achievement or, as I prefer to express it, of causing learning.

How could the time problem be resolved? Teachers who have five high school classes daily realize that their teaching duty will not be reduced to three or four classes daily. What other actions could be taken? When a school permits students to have excused absences for certain activities, the student misses a class for an activity. If there was a test given on that day, the teacher may have to create a separate makeup test and may need to supervise that student in a makeup test session one day after school. What happens if the faculty and administrators of that school listen closely to each other, to students, to parents/guardians and find a solution that reduces the number of excused absences any student could have and which says that a test cannot be missed for any activity? Let's find out.

CASE STUDY 1.1

The principal of a high school, an assistant principal, a guidance counselor, the head of each academic department, and any faculty member who chose to attend gather for the monthly Tuesday talk session at Clark High School. Tuesday talk begins at 3:45 p.m., which is fifteen minutes after school dismisses, and continues until 5:00 p.m. The agenda is established via e-mail so any adult at the school can put an item on the agenda. The agreements are (1) if you post a topic you must attend the meeting, (2) every topic and every comment must follow professional standards within education and polite, civil standards of etiquette, and (3) the discussion addresses topics, questions, ideas, problems, solutions—not people, personalities, or rumors.

BRIAN ROBERTS, PRINCIPAL: Welcome to everyone. It is 3:45. Ms. Stevens and I got here on time because the first group of buses was on time. The final few buses will be monitored by Ms. Young and Mr. Taylor, and then they will join us so all the assistant principals will be here.

Mr. Johnson posted the first topic for today's agenda, so Mr. Johnson, please lead the way.

MR. JOHNSON: The topic is how many times students are allowed to miss school. Some families take vacations during the school year, and I think there are supposed to be limits on that. Some students are absent for a week or two, come for a day, and then leave again. The truancy system is supposed to deal with them. My real concern is how many school-approved activities take students away from school. We have assemblies, theatrical performances, guest speakers that students miss class to attend. Some students are mentors at elementary schools or middle schools. Some clubs are allowed to meet during school time. We get one or two e-mails each week, it seems, with a list of students who we are supposed to excuse from class because of some meeting, activity, trip, conference, or who knows what. I know that some of those activities are important to the students, but other activities are just an easy get-out-of-class-free pass. The students cannot learn everything I teach if they are repeatedly absent. Three of my students have missed class twelve times because of every activity or meeting or project they are in. It really adds to my workload. I hope we can reduce all of these absences. Plus, the students need to be in class.

MR. EVANS: I really agree. This is my first year of teaching. I think one of the biggest surprises for me is how much I resent students coming up and saying, "Mr. Evans, I won't be in class today. Our class officers have to meet with our sponsor during her planning period to prepare everything for graduation." Can't they meet before school or after school? I was a high school student just five years ago, and I missed some classes for meetings or activities. I sure do think differently about that now. Does that mean I am getting old?

MS. PHILLIPS: No, you are a few decades from being old, but you are being very practical and realistic. Teaching is difficult enough when every student does attend, but the extra hours of working with students who miss class, get behind, have to make up a test, need to find out what we did, that gets so frustrating. I put some of that information on my school webpage, but some of it has to be done in person. Sometimes it feels like I have two jobs—I teach the students who attend today, and later I teach the students who were absent today. The truth is we have a great academic program at our high school, but we do not know how effective it could be because we allow it to be interrupted or missed so many times by so many students.

MR. ROBERTS: I understand everything you have said. Now, here's what I hear from other people. I'm the principal so every group that asks for our students to be excused from class for some activity has to present the request to me. To my knowledge, there is not a policy that addresses the topic, so I just consider each request on its merits. I say no to many requests, but, of course, teachers and students don't hear much about those. You do hear about and you do feel the impact of the requests I say yes to. Does anyone think we need a school policy on this topic?

Mr. Taylor: That might help. At least everyone could know the decision-making process and requirements. It could be one way to impose some limits. We don't want to add policy after policy, but this is a topic that our school can decide for itself and creating a policy would give everyone a chance to offer their input. I'd say yes, but since Mr. Johnson brought up the topic, what do you think? I'm an assistant principal and I work with policies all day, every day. Do you think a policy could help?

Mr. Johnson: Yes, I'd certainly be in favor of starting the policy-making process on this topic. What school committee would be the right one to develop the proposed policy? Maybe the curriculum and instruction committee would be a good choice. What does everyone think?

Mr. Roberts: Unless there is any disagreement, I'll be sure that the curriculum and instruction committee members are informed of this discussion. Of course, every committee meeting of any committee welcomes attendance by teachers, students, parents/guardians, and community members. So if this topic concerns you, be sure to attend the committee meetings when the policy idea is discussed.

The discussion in Case Study 1.1 is an example of the unique perspective that teachers bring to consideration of ideas for schools. No other person in a school can explain the impact on classroom instruction that happens when students are allowed to miss class with the same insight that only teachers can provide. Notice how efficient and inexpensive the suggestion of having a limit of students being excused from classes could be. Does it cost any money to say, "No, you may not miss class to be a mentor to a middle school student?" There is no financial cost involved. Notice how effective and directly impactful the same suggestion could be for the improvement of student achievement as measured by grades or test scores. A student who is in class ten more times instead of excused from class for those ten hours of instruction could make better grades and could do better on tests. For schools that need to get these scores up, one part of the plan could be to reduce the excused absences students are given to miss class.

Efficient, effective, no cost—many ideas that meet those three standards merit consideration. Some ideas that are heard when we listen to teachers can be implemented at no financial cost yet with many potentially good results.

To a school district official who is asked by a local community group to support the idea of carefully selected high school students being trained to serve as mentors or role models for middle school students, the benefits of another school district and community partnership could be very appealing. Because that school district official does not work in a classroom at a school, the impact that this new partnership could have on the classroom reality of teachers and students may, even if considered, not be fully realized, understood, felt, or experienced.

To a school principal who is asked by a school district official to find a way to implement the new partnership between the school district and a community group, it may be politically astute to support this request, and it may also provide some beneficial experiences for students. That principal is probably aware of the concern some teachers will have about one more activity that excuses one more group of students from attending class on certain days. Yet the principal also knows that the school district is emphasizing more community involvement in the schools.

The principal also knows that his school has set some goals for increased community involvement and increased parent/guardian involvement in the school. The principal knows of several parents who are supportive of the particular community group that made this offer of a new mentoring project.

Competing demands are common. This is the fundamental issue in economics—unlimited wants, limited resources. The school district official and the principal want to work with the community group. The resource of time is limited, and it appears that taking some students out of class occasionally is the only way to implement the proposed project. Some teachers will be very frustrated as students miss classes. Those students may have a good experience as mentors, but they will miss some classroom experiences.

Maybe the high school students could become e-mentors, meaning they communicate with middle school students electronically. Maybe some mentoring could be done before school, after school, on days when school is not in session, or during summer vacation. Maybe some requests have to be rejected politely. Maybe some community groups need to set up mentoring processes that are provided separately from schools. Maybe every decision at or about schools should have to pass the "What impact will this have on teachers, students, classroom instruction, and academic achievement?" filter before going any further.

In the research done for this book, teachers mentioned time as the greatest difficulty they face. The research base is not presented as statistically sufficient to conclude with mathematical or scientific precision that the findings would be identical with every group of teachers. The research was qualitative, and what replaces the mathematical precision that comes from hundreds or thousands of scaled responses is the depth of conviction, reflection, thought, urgency, and explanation of verbatim comments that communicate the vivid reality of classrooms. The teachers' overwhelming concern about time signals that school decisions that honestly consider the time impact of any action on teachers could be decisions that are more likely to be supported and that are more likely to be implemented effectively.

"You mean all we have to do is listen to each other and schools would improve. That's the solution? It sounds so simple. To be honest, it sounds too simple. There must be more to school improvement than increasing how much people listen to each other. Don't principals and teachers and everyone else in school or school systems already listen to each other?"

Schools are very busy, active, energetic, hurried places where phones ring, bells ring, e-mails are sent, announcements are broadcast, classes are held, meals are served, meetings are conducted, activities are attended, complaints are registered, learning is experienced, misbehavior occurs, and much more happens. The pace of school life and the increased demands on school do not support time for listening, but do add to the need of and the importance of listening.

Some teachers will make their voices heard, but the comments from those vocal teachers cannot be assumed to represent the thoughts of all teachers. Enlightened school administrators will take the time and create the methods to get continuous input from teachers. The executives of a successful restaurant company cannot sit in their offices doing paperwork, attending meetings, deciding what items will be on the menu in all restaurants within the company, and deciding all prices at each restaurant location. "Our old ovens will not cook that item fast enough to serve it in the guaranteed time we tell our customers they will get their lunch." "The competition across the street just lowered prices. We have to offer some coupons or discounts or price reductions even if we are the only restaurant in the company that has this situation." The success that comes from improved communications in corporate America can also come from improved communications in classroom America.

"But it takes time to communicate, to listen." It saves time. Investing one hour to identify the reality in the classrooms of a school can prevent weeks, months, years of bad ideas being imposed on those classrooms. Listening to teachers is smart, efficient, proper, enlightened, and fully consistent with the ultimate leadership, management, people-skill guideline—"Do unto others as you would have them do unto you" (Matthew 7:12).

In addition to time concerns, what other insight into the classroom reality does the research provide? Get comfortable, prepare your brain to think profound thoughts, and please thoroughly read the following verbatim comments. As we read these comments we are listening to teachers, so please think about the insights these sample comments provide about what actions could be most effective in supporting teachers and what actions, despite good intentions, could actually be counterproductive.

1. "What are the most difficult parts of your job as a teacher?" As previously indicated, the most common answer was time. Motivation of students, dealing with uncooperative parents/guardians, and disciplining students were the other most frequently mentioned topics.

- "The actual hardest part of my job is motivating and working with students who do not have a vision of success. They may hate school, reject intellectual pursuits, or have an image of 'cool' that does not involve success at school. I think this largely comes from a separate culture that teens have developed apart from the life of adults."
- "Managing the behavior of students who act out to an extreme."
- "Dealing with behavior problem students and nonsupportive parents."
- "Working with parents who do not hold their children accountable for their actions and choices."
- "Dealing with extreme behavior problems in the classroom on a daily basis."

2. "During your career as a teacher, what has changed the most about the job that has increased the difficulty?"

- "Parents are more willing to make excuses for their child today. This makes discipline and rule enforcement more challenging."
- "Our field is no longer viewed as a service field, but a product one. The responsibilities of the student to learn and of the parent to correct behavior are no longer expected. The teacher is to produce learning regardless of the situation."
- "There are more excuses for student nonperformance, such as disorders or syndromes that have a questionable basis but that are used as excuses. This is at the same time we have increased demands for higher test scores."
- "Test scores have become a reflection on the teacher rather than the students. The focus is now on testing and not really on learning."
- "The pressure from the administration increases each year with expectations for high test scores."
- "More and more paperwork."
- "The increase in the number of students and parents not being satisfied with the amount I reach out to them. I send out an e-mail with study guides and other information, but they complain about it when they get it."
- "More non-classroom-related demands."
- "The paperwork and the pressures of the No Child Left Behind law."
- "The biggest change is the focus on the individual student. I think this is a great change, and I have shifted my teaching practices. There is a time cost involved with this—it takes more time."

3. "What are you asked to do now as a teacher that ten or twenty years ago teachers were not asked to do, expected to do, or required to do?"

- "Accommodate whatever ridiculous requests parents make, pass students who do not work."
- "One of the hardest is to not inconvenience the parent. We should be at their beck and call but should not bother them at home or work. We should not accuse their child of any misbehavior unless we have incontrovertible proof."
- "We are unofficial parents. This year I bought clothes for students in need, and I helped get prom attire."

THE CLASSROOM REALITY

- "Follow an instructional scripted program that allows no creativity."
- "There are no ability-level groups, so teachers are expected to differentiate instruction to low, average, and gifted children all in one short class period."
- "Being more data driven. It's not just about making gains that before would have been acceptable. Now if proficiency is not reached, credit is not given for the gains made. Also, the demands on teachers have increased to the rapid burnout level."
- "Attending so much required professional development training that is not related to what I teach or who I teach."
- "Teachers today are expected to put up with students' ugly behavior because all of the kids have problems. So we just have to put up with it—no consequences ever seem to be fully carried out. Fewer kids have responsibility."
- "Make exceptions for students who refuse to do homework, study, or behave."
- "Considering the needs of the individual child is much bigger than before. Also, there are much more expectations beyond the regular school day such as meetings and training where attendance is required."

Pause for a moment to reflect on the above comments from teachers. What are some of the most frequently mentioned topics? Are those the topics that school administrators, school district superintendents, community groups, political leaders, lawmakers, policy makers, school board members, or education bureaucrats would mention? Fully resolving every issue named by teachers is unlikely. Listening to teachers is possible and is necessary. Having the courage and the desire to improve a school includes having the wisdom to identify the real problems, to listen to the people who do the most vital work, and form the plan that addresses the most vital concerns.

4. "What causes you the most frustration or disappointment in your job as a teacher?"

The reader might expect answers to this question to emphasize teacher pay, the number of students in each class, vouchers, or other topics commonly considered by the media or by political leaders when the topic is education. The teachers who participated in the survey research for this book had other ideas, many of which are not a function of money or of laws but of what is done in schools, of how that is done, of how people are treated, and of whether learning really is the top priority.

- "The lack of respect that I feel parents and the general public have for teachers."
- "There is so much to do and so little time. The focus is on test scores and not on meeting the individual needs of each and every student."
- "Seeing students fail is the most distressing feeling. Some students have enormous barriers they can't seem to overcome for a variety of reasons. Many of these are low socioeconomic students. It is terribly sad and tragic to see students who come from a poor background fail in school and know that another generation of struggling on the edge of middle class or lower is beginning. The role of substance abuse in this is huge. There really is a perpetual underclass developing in our society."
- "Misconceptions of our job."
- "The one or two kids each year who seem to make their personal mission to disrupt the order of our class."
- "Parents who do not support decisions that teachers make."
- "Lots of concentration on what teachers are doing wrong and little praise for what we do right."
- "The same students cause problems day after day, year after year. No consequences seem to matter, and there is not an alternative school to send them to."
- "Constant behavior problems that take away from instructional time."
- "Not being recognized for the extra jobs I do. Not being able to reach a student."
- "The criticism when test scores are released. We get little praise for the hard work."
- "Lack of support and/or encouragement from school and district leadership."
- "Switching to the newest methods without giving last year's newest method a chance to produce results."

THE CLASSROOM REALITY

- "Students who are utterly unmotivated because their home environments don't show them a reason to get an education."
- "Parents who defend their children no matter what."

5. "What would you like to tell people who think that teaching is easy work done on an easy schedule about the day-to-day reality of teaching?"

- "That most days I go in at 7:30 a.m. and stay until 6:00 p.m. and that my 'jobless' summer is spent in training and doing a second job to make ends meet."
- "Come try it for one day!"
- "Try it."
- "7:40 a.m.–5:00 p.m. plus professional development programs plus faculty meetings plus meetings for students with special needs plus after-school events to attend plus papers to grade and grades to enter in the computer."
- "Teaching is mentally and emotionally draining. If all students were from good families who had values then maybe it would be easy. We have lots of students at many different ability levels and we are responsible for getting all of them up to the same required level of achievement."
- "Teaching is probably the most challenging thing I have ever done. Several demands come from every direction. Some seem impossible or overwhelming."
- "I would tell them to try it for a day and see what they feel about it. I'd also say that it is not about if it is easy or hard, but the feeling that I've made a difference in someone's life."
- "You try it and then we'll see what you have to say."
- "The amount of time spent after school without compensation would easily fill the nonwork days of the summer."
- "Our job has a mentally exhausting element that few jobs have."
- "Come to school one day with a prepared lesson that you teach five different times to students whose favorite phrase is 'this sucks.' Assess their learning and accept total responsibility for any failures."

6. "What would you like to tell people who make laws or policies about education—school board members, state legislators, governors, members of congress, the president—about the day-to-day reality of teaching?"

- "That we as teachers want what is best for our students and that we deserve the respect and freedom to make decisions about what is needed."
- "They need to spend a lot of time observing in schools, speaking to teachers and students, and relying on that information when it is time to make decisions."
- "Your tests and test data are meaningless."
- "Quit trying to micromanage. Don't demand accountability of us that you wouldn't want imposed on yourself."
- "We work so hard. We buy school materials with our own money. We don't have enough help or time to get it all done before the annual assessment. Visit a classroom for a week."
- "Spend a day in some schools, meet with the teachers."
- "Not all students have the same ability. A true measure would be testing students at the beginning of the year and again at the end. Compare them and if they have improved, great. They should be compared against themselves."
- "Parents and families should be held more accountable. Teachers are held solely responsible for achievement."
- "Test scores don't always show everything a child has learned. Teaching isn't just about content, but life skills."
- "They need to talk with educators in the classroom before making many of these decisions. What may sound great on paper may not work in the classroom."
- "Professionals who have left the classroom do not remember the reality of what we do. What looks good on paper, in theory may sound good, but often reality won't work that way."
- "Educators cannot solve every problem society creates."

Now, please reflect about those verbatim comments. Are those teachers asking for salary increases? Are those teachers asking for new laws, policies, regulations, or procedures? Are those teachers eager to share

THE CLASSROOM REALITY   15

their insights? Are those teachers asking that decision makers listen to them, understand the classroom reality in which they work, and trust teachers more to provide information, ideas, and input before decisions are made?

•

CASE STUDY 1.2

This case study is set in a conference room at a middle school. The school's principal is retiring effective with the end of the current school year. The group of very interested people meeting in the conference is the interviewing committee made up of six members: the retiring principal, three teachers, two parents of students currently attending seventh grade at this middle school, which has grades six, seven, and eight.

MS. SANDERS: Well, is everyone ready for our final interview? We've had five candidates so far, and we have one more person to interview. We all know the prepared questions, so if everyone is ready I'll get Mr. VanMeter who will be the last person we interview. [Ms. Sanders brings Mr. VanMeter into the conference room, introduces everyone, and asks the first question.] Mr. VanMeter, we have read your résumé, and we know that you have experience. Now, we have a list of twelve prepared questions. Each person on the committee will ask you two questions. Of course, other follow-up questions may emerge as we hear your answers. We will have time at the end for you to ask us questions. Let's start. Please tell us about your decision-making process.

MR. VANMETER: I listen to people. I intend to visit every classroom every day during first period one day, second period the next day, and so on in a continuous sequence. I'll be in the hallways at class change time. I'll read all e-mails and reply to them. I'll attend committee meetings, and I'll attend some of the school's task force meetings. I will be in the office when necessary and everywhere else in the school building whenever possible. I'll call a few families each day to keep in touch, to get input, to hear concerns. I'll have one lunchtime open forum per month for any student to talk with me and one after-school forum each month for teachers and staff to talk with me. In areas where I make the decision, I will get vast input, if time permits, and then decide. Topics of immediate urgency will get much faster consideration and input as time or urgency permit. In areas where decision making is shared, I'll lead by example so everyone listens to each other and then a decision is made.

MR. GORDON, TEACHER: Mr. VanMeter, our school is accustomed to making decisions based on data. So the question I have is how will you use data to make decisions?

MR. VANMETER: When data is helpful we will use it, assuming it is accurate, valid, and reliable. Some statistic that says the school scored eighty-three on some measurement tells you absolutely nothing about any student or any teacher at the school. The daily grades the student earns in a class tell us much more about the student than a state or national test taken by the student during a two-hour testing session in early May. To be honest, schools that are obsessed with data concern me. My magnificent obsessions are students, teachers, and learning. Some of what happens in school can be expressed in numbers, but not every part of education is quantifiable. I'm here for real learning, not for the slice of learning that an annual state-required or national government–required test tries to measure.

How do you think this interview is going so far? What do the questions reveal about the school, and what do the answers reveal about Mr.VanMeter? What is the likelihood that Mr. VanMeter will be selected for this job? First, write what you think the next ten questions will be, and think of the answers you expect Mr. VanMeter to give. Second, read the provided ending and evaluate how that ending matches with the conclusion you expected.

3.   8.
4.   9.
5.   10.
6.   11.
7.   12.

MS. SANDERS: Our time is running out, Mr. VanMeter. You have answered all of our prepared questions, and we have answered several questions you had for us. Is there anything else you would like to say?

MR. VANMETER: Just this. If your first priority is students, we agree. If your magnificent obsession is for classrooms to be productive places where teachers cause learning, we agree. If you are looking for a principal who is a bureaucrat, a police officer, a yes-man, and a best friend to everyone, please select someone else. If you are looking for a principal who will help lead this school so every student learns and every teacher has meaningful career experiences, we can work together. I do not bring a formula, a prescription, or a fill-in-the-blank trendy scheme for school improvement. I bring an eagerness to listen to everyone, work with everyone, and together create the school of our shared dreams. Thanks for this opportunity to meet with you. I will eagerly await your decision.

Did Mr. VanMeter get the job? If you answer yes, what were the reasons he was selected? If you answer no, what were those reasons?

CASE STUDY 1.3

PAULA: Nobody listens to us. We know more about school than anyone else. I'd like to see the governor come teach my classes for a week. He would beg for mercy. He has an easy job sitting in his fancy office with a staff of people to help him with anything he needs. I don't have a staff, and I don't have an office, but I get my job done in the classroom better than the governor gets his job done.

Faculty lounge conversations can be on any subject within the total range of topics related to education and on some subjects beyond education. Today the topic during lunch has become why teachers are not involved more in the decisions that impact classrooms. Let's listen to the rest of this conversation of high school teachers.

MITCHELL: Here's my complaint. The national government and the state government have passed laws telling us how much progress our students must make each year. If that progress does not happen, we get pounded with blame and criticism. I'd like to see the government live up to standards like that. Hey, every year the national government has a financial deficit is a year we don't have to reach our No Child Left Behind goals. Let's see how the president and congress like that.

CELESTE: I've taught here for nineteen years. I've heard this conversation before. Teachers always feel like nobody listens to them, but how much effort do we really make to be heard? Do we attend school board meetings? Do we attend our school improvement plan task force meetings? Do we e-mail ideas and comments to the principal? Do we ever tell the governor what we think, or do we just let it go with a discussion during lunch?

THOMAS: Good point, and I'll accept the challenge. The school improvement task force meets tomorrow after school. The principal, an assistant principal, a school counselor, the department heads of each academic subject will be there. Any teacher is invited. I'll go. I'll speak up. What should I say on your behalf?

ANDREA: Here's what you could say for me. Tell everyone that what matters is teaching and learning and students. Tell them to tell the people at central office to get out of their offices and come spend time at school. I get so fed up with central office people telling us what to do. I should be telling the central office people what to do. Their job should be to help me do my job, not to send me endless e-mails about meetings to attend or paperwork to complete. Tell them that for me.

ELLEN: I agree with Andrea, only my emphasis is the state education bureaucrats who are so far removed from school and the reality of teaching that they must think what matters most are policies and regulations instead of students and learning. Here's my theory. Central office people are 50 percent out of touch and 50 percent in touch with classroom reality. So if two central office people talk to each other about education you get 50 percent times 50 percent, which is 25 percent of reality. They take each other further from reality than they each were when their conversation began. State education bureaucrats are 90 percent removed from reality, so if two central office people talk to one state education bureaucrat, the result is 50 percent times 50 percent times 10 percent. That's 2.5 percent of reality. No wonder teachers get frustrated. We know 100 percent of the classroom reality. We are face-to-face daily with 100 percent of the classroom reality. People who make decisions that impact us are far removed from the classroom reality.

THOMAS: So do I tell the task force that central office people and state government education bureaucrats are the problem? Is that fair? Is that a bit simplistic, or is it accurate?

ROBIN: I've been listening. I can answer your question, Thomas. Yes, it's fair, or, at least, it is the perception many people have. Once a person leaves the classroom and goes to do any other job in education, they quickly lose the impact of or the reality of working in classrooms. I know that many of those people mean well and have good intentions, but some of them are power hungry or don't like working with students or just wanted to make more money or realized they could not function in the classroom any longer. The only people who work in education who really know today's classroom reality are teachers. Nothing should be done in education without thorough input from teachers. Every decision needs to go through a teacher impact analysis to see if what is being considered is helpful, is possible, is necessary as far as it relates to teachers doing their jobs with students and for students. Does that make sense?

Well, reader, what do you think—does that make sense? What could be the benefits to education in general and to each classroom in particular if all decisions related to schools went through the very precise filter of "Is this helpful to teachers, is this possible for teachers to do, is this necessary or not?"

Teaching and learning in classrooms are the essence of what matters most in schools. Education is not about new, expanded, circuitous, procedural, multilayered bureaucracies. Education is not about massive, systemic, top-down organizational reforms. Education is not about restructuring of the state government educational bureaucracy or of a school district's central office bureaucracy. Education is about teaching and learning, which means that education is about teachers and students, which means that education is about the reality in classrooms. Dealing directly with that reality every day is what teachers do. No other educator, bureaucrat, political leader, community activist, advocacy group member, or citizen deals directly with the classroom reality all day, every day. The most accurate insights about the classroom reality will come from the person who daily endeavors to make that reality the best it can be—the classroom teacher. Listen to teachers. Hear their unique insight. Accept their input as having a singular characteristic that no other input can provide—it's based on the current classroom reality.

Basing all efforts to improve education on the accurate understanding of the current classroom reality is sensible, efficient, humane, and long overdue. Central office workers and state or national education bureaucrats usually care about schools and usually expect themselves to do their job well. The level of concern and the work ethic are not the issues here. The issue is that a sincere desire to improve education requires caring enough to emphasize listening to the people who have the vital, essential, pivotal duty in education, and that is teachers.

Teachers uniquely know the classroom reality; therefore, everyone involved with education and/or seeking to impact education must listen to teachers. Insights, ideas, and complaints gained from that listening must be acknowledged, taken seriously, given high priority, and, whenever possible and beneficial, acted upon.

The cure for problems that are within the current classroom reality begins with total awareness of the classroom reality. That awareness makes it clear, obvious, and certain what changes would be helpful and what changes are not needed.

Let's move on. What is a very common statement made to teachers by anyone who is not a teacher? My experience is that the most likely comment is "I don't see how you do that," meaning people do not see how teachers endure teaching. Since many teachers prevail, persist, and actually thrive on teaching, it will be their honor to reply to the statement "I don't see how you do that." The next chapter explores that topic.

2

THE ISSUE

I Don't See How You Do That

That's the problem. You do not see how I teach because you do not see me teach. You rarely, if ever, see any teachers teach day after day, class after class.

What do you see? Meetings; presentations at state and national conferences, conventions, or workshops; reports, charts, graphs, executive summaries of data collections; magazines and journals about education; national, state, and local reports about schools. Studies done by interest groups. Reports issued by think tanks. Minutes of meetings. Forms to fill out. Legislative testimony. Press conferences.

You do not see me teach. You do not see Tasha, Shawn, or other students in my classes. How can you lead, manage, or make decisions well if you do not see the reality in classrooms?

Oh, you walk through two classrooms per day, per week, per month, or per year. You stay for five minutes per walk-through and get a quick view of 1 percent of my day. Why rely on something so superficial, so bureaucratic, so limited? Just because you took notes on some handheld electronic device during your five-minute walk-through does not make your visit any better. You can do your job better by fully understanding the reality of my job.

You see the number eighty-seven, which the company that designed the test being used this year tells you means something has improved because last year the number was eighty-five. Last year's test was provided by a different company and had a slightly different test design, but your well-paid test consultants and statisticians tell you that the mathematical processes to relate one score to another score have been completed according to accepted test protocols.

The eighty-seven number is related to how high school juniors did on the social studies part of the test. Now, tell me, how did Tasha do on the test? How did Shawn do? Did so many students do well that the score increased by two points versus last year even though some students this year had very low scores?

I can tell you about Tasha and Shawn. I teach them every day. I know if they can answer today's questions. I know their score on our tests, projects, homework, and quizzes. I can tell you what works best when Tasha or Shawn encounters some problem. I can tell you their career goals, their hobbies, their learning strengths, and their personalities. I can tell you that Shawn's family e-mails his teachers monthly for a progress report. I can tell you that Tasha's family checks her grades via Internet weekly. I can tell you more about Tasha and Shawn than any report, article, executive summary, or meeting can tell you about students.

I realize that you don't see how I do my job as a teacher. You don't see, understand, realize, or appreciate everything it takes for a teacher to do the classroom teaching job well. You have your duties somewhere in the maze of the education bureaucracy or somewhere in the battleground of local, state, and national politics. You are very busy with meetings, reports, conferences, workshops, and papers.

The truth is, I don't see how you do your job. How can you endure another day of meetings and more meetings, of reports to issue, of absolutely pointless conference presentations to hear? The work of education that matters most is done in classrooms. The percentage of your time that is spent in classrooms or spent listening to people who work in classrooms and the weight you give that input in your decisions indicates to you the percentage of your effort that is based on direct knowledge of Tasha, Shawn, their teachers, and their reality.

Do yourself an incredible favor. Come to school. Visit classrooms. Sit down and watch, listen, observe, stay all morning, all afternoon, all day. Repeat this often.

Why is this a gift, a favor you can give yourself? The next meeting you have to attend will not need to be two hours of the same old bureaucratic review of reports, charts, graphs, and executive summaries from the national, state, and local department of redundancy. The next meeting will be completed in fifteen minutes because instead of two hours' worth of repetitious chatter, you will bring the powerful, penetrating, and life-giving liberation of reality. The meeting can get to the point because now you get the point, which is what can be done to support, help, enhance the classroom reality that Tasha, Shawn, and teachers are experiencing.

If you work in education but are not a classroom teacher, or if you seek to impact education but are not a classroom teacher, maybe you are one of the enlightened leaders who already spend a significant amount of time in classrooms. You know the importance, the benefits, the efficiency of experiencing the classroom reality and of listening to teachers. Please tell your colleagues to follow your example. If you have the authority, please require your colleagues to get into classrooms often.

Let's read what some of the survey participants wrote in response to this very directly related question: "Some people say to teachers about the work that teachers do at schools, 'I don't see how you do that.' How do you do this job that other people cannot imagine doing?"

- "I do it because I love the kids, and I recognize that because I can do this job, I must do it because it is so important and no one else can even imagine doing it."
- "I like working with kids. I think they are fun and energetic. Mostly their immature silliness does not bother me."
- "Because it is my passion."
- "I often wonder how I do it. Some days, especially if a parent is upset with me, I doubt if I have what it takes. But I made a commitment to improve so I keep at it."
- "God-given patience."
- "Teaching is an innate quality that people possess just like medical professionals (I couldn't imagine doing that!) or any profession. Teachers who make it to full retirement were born to teach."
- "I guess it's almost like a survival mechanism kicks in gear. You do it because you have to. You learn to multitask and get organized enough to complete the tasks at hand."

- "It's hard, but you do it."
- "I try my best at everything and tell myself every day that it is about the kids, not all of the paperwork."
- "I do this job because I have been called to use my talents to teach."
- "I have patience—I can think on my feet. I can see many situations from the kid's point of view. I always remember that they are children and will mess up."
- "I genuinely love the subject I teach, and I want to share it with young people."

Those comments are from teachers, not from people who used to teach or from people who are otherwise involved in efforts to impact education. What do teachers know about school that no other person knows? Each teacher knows the reality within his or her classroom. Notice how earnestly the above comments communicate the commitment the quoted teachers have to improving the classroom reality, the classroom experience for their students. Teachers have this unique awareness of the classroom reality, and teachers are in the unique position to have a direct, daily, minute-to-minute impact on that reality. Teachers directly impact students; therefore, teachers have the most vital, the most important, the most potentially productive position in education for causing learning. For those reasons every effort to improve education must include vast input from and support from teachers. Is that what usually happens? Let's explore some common circumstances.

CASE STUDY 2.1

The two major political party candidates for governor in a state meet one week prior to the election for their final televised debate. It has been agreed that one major topic of this debate will be education because no part of the state budget is larger than the cost of education. After the standard introductions and opening comments, the two candidates reply to the question, "How will you improve education in our state?"

MR. WILSON: Our schools will become the best in the nation, the best in the world. My campaign has already proposed the Total Education Adjustments Change Humans plan, or as it is usually called, TEACH. We have to totally adjust what we do in education and how we do it. In my job as lieutenant governor during the past eight years, I have served as the governor's liaison to education. I have attended many international and national conferences on schools. I served on the U.S. Department of Education task force study group committee, which reviewed data from every state department of education in our country. Our committee reviewed over twenty-five hundred pages of data from the fifty states. I know the statistics on education because there were seven hundred charts in those twenty-five hundred pages. I know what other states are doing to improve their schools. I can bring the best ideas from all over the nation and implement those ideas in schools throughout our state.

MS. WESLEYAN: I have served on a local school board. I have made important decisions about schools and the policies they need. I have been a member of our state's house of representatives and of our state's senate. I have introduced over one hundred bills in my career as a legislator, and twelve of those bills were about education. I have served on three different education reform task force blue-ribbon-committee restructuring study groups that advised the governor on new laws, regulations, and policies needed for our schools. I know how the legislative process works so I can get the results our schools need.

MODERATOR: Both of you have mentioned your commitment to education. Now, tell us please how much time you have spent in public school classrooms in our state during the past year? Mr. Wilson, let's begin with you.

MR. WILSON: That's a very good question. Here's how I look at it. Our teachers and our school administrators are in the schools every day doing their vital work. I'm in our state capital attending important meetings and working with other state leaders. I travel the state meeting with local officials to get their input on many issues including education. I did attend a ground-breaking ceremony for a new high school being built in Newbern County, so I go everywhere I can to support our schools.

MS. WESLEYAN: I've been to three ground-breaking ceremonies in the past year, one for a new elementary school, one for a new middle school, and one for a new high school. My campaign's website has pictures from each of those ceremonies. I have perfect attendance throughout my legislative career for each education committee or subcommittee I have served on. When it comes to schools, no other candidate can match the time or effort I have invested and will invest.

MODERATOR: Just to be clear, neither of you have been in a classroom of a public school in this state during the past year.

MR. WILSON: That is correct.

MS. WESLEYAN: I was scheduled to speak to a high school U.S. history class last February, but school was cancelled that day due to snow, so I wanted to go, but the bad weather prevented it.

Neither candidate for governor in that fictional debate had been in a public school classroom in the past year, yet both candidates were absolutely certain that they had the ideas, the knowledge, the political skill, the political experience, the commitment needed to make significant educational improvements in their state. That is unrealistic and illogical. No doubt, Mr. Wilson and Ms. Wesleyan have important experience and skill that could be applied toward efforts to improve education. No doubt their schedules in the past year were busy. No doubt their broad, generic, lofty statements about education can make impressive campaign materials, slogans, promises, or press releases. No doubt teachers know much more about the classroom reality than Mr. Wilson or Ms. Wesleyan know. How could the knowledge of teachers and the political skill of Ms. Wesleyan or Mr. Wilson be combined to make educational improvements?

Mr. Wilson and Ms. Wesleyan or any other political leader, school board member, school district central office worker, or community leader who would improve education must spend some time in classrooms and must spend more time listening to teachers. How is this done? There are many possible ways, so let's explore several options.

CASE STUDY 2.2

"It has been an amazing day. Thank you for welcoming me to your school today. I visited twelve classrooms and stayed for thirty minutes in each room. Your block schedule worked very well for many purposes. I visited three classes per block. I saw classes at each high school grade level. I know, it is only one day. I will be back. For now, I'll listen to your faculty meeting discussion, and then anyone who would like to stay and talk with me after the faculty meeting is welcome to do that." Ms. Vickie Simpson works in the state education department, office of high school improvement. She spends two or three days per week in schools, in classrooms. She is in touch with her office by phone or by e-mail. She is in touch with teachers, students, and school administrators in person through her visits. She has been given one major assignment for this school year—go to the schools, listen to educators, find out what the real issues are, see what they are up against, hear from them about what they need, determine what they feel prevents them from getting the results they seek, understand their challenges and their achievements, compile a realistic, precise, blunt, and actionable report at the end of the year about what schools need and what they do not need.

At the end of the year, Ms. Simpson presented the following report to the state commissioner of education and to the state school board:

> A mistake has been made. The mistake was not intentional. The mistake can be corrected. The mistake was to think that school would improve if only the educational bureaucracy, laws, regulations, policies, task forces, committees, study groups, procedures, rules, and reforms could be perfected. Education is not about all of those organizational endeavors. Education is about students, teachers, and what they do in classrooms.
>
> Taxes are necessary. Laws are necessary. Policies, rules, and regulations are necessary, but too often all of those seem to become the priority. Students, teachers, and what they do in classrooms are the priority.
>
> I have visited over 120 high schools in the past year. I have closely observed in over eleven hundred high school classrooms during the past year. I have talked with over two thousand high school teachers in the past year. I have talked with over five hundred high school administrators, counselors, social workers, and staff members in the past year. Their commitment is impressive, their concerns are serious. In some way they need us to do more. In other ways they need us to do much less. Here are details of what I heard and saw.
>
> 1. Teaching has become a much more demanding, complicated, exhausting job than you or I realized. We are responsible for some of the

complications imposed by bureaucracy. We can provide support to help address the real needs of teachers.

2. We must get more direct input from teachers and from school administrators before we make any changes in anything the state requires. To be blunt, teachers and principals are convinced that people who work in the state government's education department have no idea of what it is like to work in a school today. Teachers and principals are also very concerned that people who work in their local school district's central office are not fully aware of what working at a school requires.

3. When we do not hear from teachers we are far too likely to interpret that silence as satisfaction with or agreement with what state laws, policies, or regulations demand. Wrong. Few teachers communicate with us because they have concluded that such communication is a waste of time.

4. The teachers I observed and talked to are working hard, care a lot about doing their job well, and put in more hours than you or I realize. The same conclusions apply to principals.

5. There's one conclusion I did not expect. Many high school teachers told me how frustrating it is for coaches and athletes at school to get a lot of attention, rewards, and recognition while good teachers and successful students get much less attention.

6. The teachers generally tolerate the annual testing that our state requires. They work to prepare students for the tests, and they very carefully monitor the test-taking sessions. Here's the other part of this subject—they do not believe that the tests are accurate, valid, or reliable. They also think that the major emphasis on tests is a distraction from real learning. Plus, the time given to taking tests is time lost from instruction. Some students seem to think that once the annual tests are completed the rest of the school year is not very important. The teachers really resent that a few days of test taking create sets of results that are used as the ultimate measure of how well a school is doing.

7. One more conclusion—teachers are very resentful of the increased involvement of the national government in education. Teachers and principals told me that it is impossible for the national government to effectively micromanage education throughout this country. The truth is, many of the educators I met thought that the state government interfered too much with the education work local people were doing in their communities where the local people know their problems and needs better than anyone else.

What responses would state school board members offer after hearing that report? Responses would range from "The law is the law, and like it or not the people in our schools have to do what the laws and regulations and policies require" to "We have to take these findings seriously. Without the total commitment of teachers and principals to any effort to improve schools, not much will change." Some people who heard the report might wonder what could be done to create some harmonious cooperation among everyone involved in education from the teacher to the principal to the local school district officials to the local school board to the state department of education to the state legislature to the governor and then to the national government. Community groups, interest groups, lobbyists, political parties, and civic advocates/reformers also seek to impact education. What, if anything, could possibly unify these many people so there is less friction, frustration, or failure and more student achievement?

To help answer that question a look at the education universe is needed. How can some mutual understanding be created between people who look at the work teachers do and remark, "I don't see how you do that" and teachers who look at everyone else in the education universe with wonder asking, "Why don't you realize how difficult my job is, how hard I am working, and how much it means to me to do this job well?" First, we will explore the range of participants in education. Then we will think about how to better connect these varied members.

The center of the education universe is the classroom. Or is it? The center of the education universe can sometimes seem to be the national government in Washington, D.C., or any state government in the fifty respective state capital cities.

What happens in the classroom is more important than what happens at any other place in the education universe. Presidents, governors, members of the U.S. Congress, state legislators, school board members at the state or local levels, department of education employees at the national or state levels, school district central office workers at the local level all are concerned about education, all can or do have some impact on education, but none of those people work in classrooms, which is where education happens. The classroom is and must be treated as the center of the education universe. The classroom must be the top priority of the education universe. What teachers and students do in the classroom is the essence of education.

If we get the classroom right, we get education right. If we do not get the classroom right, nothing else in the education universe can make up for that.

Consider these categories of people, in table 2.1, who are involved in or with education. For the purpose of this book, the emphasis is on how and/or whether groups 1, 2, 3, and 4 work together toward the shared purpose of continuously improving the classroom experience of students and teachers. Also, the emphasis in this book is that people in group 1—teachers—have a unique duty, perspective, and insight about the essential work of education, truly the purpose of education, which is to cause learning. The premise of this book further contends that people in groups 2, 3, and 4 do their job best when they are most supportive of, most in touch with, and most aware of the realities faced by teachers.

Teachers are direct educators. Teachers are face-to-face with students. Teachers are the people in the education universe who have the greatest likelihood of causing the improved academic achievement results by students, which everyone supports. Of course, every request made by a teacher cannot be guaranteed, and every complaint expressed by teachers cannot be resolved. Still, teachers are the only people in the education universe who can provide the most accurate, the most current, the most realistic, the most useful, and the most personal information about the reality of the classroom.

Table 2.1

1.	Teachers	Direct Educators
2.	Principals	Managerial Educators
	Assistant Principals	
	School Counselors	
	Other School Support Staff	
3.	School District Central Office Personnel	Organizational Educators
	School Board Members	
	State Department of Education Personnel	
	State School Board Members	
4.	Public Officials	Education Influentials and Social Reformers
	Interest Groups	
	Advocacy Groups	
	Media	
5.	Students	Education Partners and Beneficiaries
6.	Parents/Guardians	Education Clients
	Taxpayers	
	Citizens	

THE ISSUE

Managerial educators include principals, assistant principals, school counselors, school social workers, school law enforcement officers, and other school support staff. These managerial educators work in school buildings but do not work in classrooms all day, every day. Principals and assistant principals do spend some time in classrooms, do some work with individual students or groups of students, do much work with teachers or groups of teachers. Managerial educators have responsibility for all or part of what happens in a school but cannot take direct action or have direct face-to-face interaction with all students. Managerial educators have important work to do that is done best when always designed to provide the highest quantity of and the highest quality of support for the work done in the classroom.

Who are the organizational educators? They are school district central office personnel, school board members, state department of education personnel, and state school board members. These people do not work at a school. Some of these people work full-time within a large education organization while others work in elected or appointed school board positions. These people spend very little time in classrooms. These people spend a lot of time in offices and in meetings. Organizational educators make and/or help implement decisions, policies, and regulations that impact schools. To the extent that organizational educators do spend time in classrooms and do get input from teachers, their decisions, policies, and regulations are more likely to address classroom realities and therefore to support teachers in their direct work with students.

Education influentials and social reformers are public officials including the president, members of congress, governors, and state legislators. Also in the category of education influentials and social reformers are members or leaders of interest groups, advocacy groups, and community groups.

The people in these four groups have very different jobs to do. Recall that the research responses included some teachers who eagerly invited others in the education universe—managerial, organizational, influentials, social reformers—to come occasionally and do the work of a classroom teacher to be reminded of or, for the first time, to be fully aware of the realities of being a classroom teacher. Teachers are asking more people to come see what the job of teacher really is today. Teachers would appreciate the effort to understand and acknowledge their work. The people visiting the classroom could then do their managerial, organizational, influential, or reform work more accurately, more realistically, more efficiently, more effectively, more humanely—everyone wins!

What are some of the differences in the jobs done by direct educators—teachers—and by other people in the education universe? Teachers think of individual students. When discussing education, teachers know individual students and their grades, class participation, personality, career interest, and extracurricular activities. Most other people in the education universe do not talk about individual students, but about groups of students at the school building level, at the school district level, at the state level or the national level. Teachers know individual students. Managerial educators know some individual students, but part or much of their work is done with the aggregate of a school's student body or with a sizable group within that student body.

Concepts versus realities of implementation. Generalities versus individualized specifics. Students as demographic groups versus students as individuals with whom you work day to day. Social goals versus individual student progress. Achievement and results are caused by law, policies, regulations, and organizational restructuring versus achievement, and results are caused by teachers daily teaching students in classrooms.

The pairs in the above paragraph show a dichotomy within the education universe of people who do not work in classrooms and people who do work in classrooms. The goal may be similar, such as improved achievement; however, the preferred ways to reach that goal are different.

If you work as a teacher in a classroom your job is to cause learning. If you are a managerial educator, your job description and your job evaluation place emphasis on how well you manage the parts of the school for which you have responsibility. If you are an organizational educator your job description and your job evaluation place emphasis on how well you complete tasks for the organization whether those tasks impact classrooms or merely help the bureaucracy function. If you are an education influential or a social reformer, your job description may be measured in how much media attention you get or how much power brokering you can do.

There is another aspect to the "I don't see how you do that" inquiry. That aspect is, "Why don't you see how I do that? Why don't you come to my classroom and see how I do this? Why don't you ask me how I do this job of teaching or what I need to make this job accomplish all we hope it will do?"

Such communication is possible, does happen in some places, and can happen in more places. How?

CASE STUDY 2.3

PRINCIPAL: Something went wrong. Somewhere in the past decade or two, something went wrong. That's why I called this meeting of our school's management team. I've been thinking lately that the goals I had when I became a teacher and the goals that I had when I became a school administrator are not what I spend my time on now as principal of this school. Answering questions from central office people or completing reports for the school board or updating some records for the state department of education or trying to figure out how to obey and implement some new law—it's all so far removed from the goals of doing what is best for students.

ASSISTANT PRINCIPAL: Paperwork, paperwork, paperwork. All of us are covered with stacks of paperwork. We are supposed to work with students, teachers, staff members, but we work with paper or with the computer screen version of what used to be paper.

GUIDANCE COUNSELOR: What choices do we have? There are 1,872 students in this high school. Most of them do what they are supposed to do most of the time. Then some student causes a major problem in room 255, and it could take two adults working the rest of the day to get that resolved. And that incident will add to the paperwork because there will be reports to write. I spend 95 percent of my time on 5 percent of the students I am responsible for. Each counselor has four hundred to five hundred students we are supposed to know, to advise, to meet with, to help, to counsel. How can that be done?

SECURITY OFFICER: It's the same for us. Ideally, the officers would prevent problems. We would be all over the hallways and the campus. We would see the students who skip class and deal with them immediately before they make a bigger mistake. We would prevent vandalism. We would monitor any student who is court involved. As it is, we barely keep up with every emergency that happens. One incident can take hours and hours to investigate. It really bothers me when something bad happens to a student who never causes any trouble. You know, the student who is here every day, on time to every class, makes good grades, gets involved in school activities, and then some teenage criminal steals that student's books or money or something else. We've asked for security cameras to be installed everywhere in the school, but who listens to that idea? The central office people who reject that idea don't work in a school building and seem to be out of touch with the reality we deal with. I guess nothing ever gets stolen at central office so they don't feel much sympathy for us.

TEACHER: I really can't speak for every teacher, but I can tell you how many teachers I hear talking about leaving this profession. This work is just not what they expected it to be. They planned to be teachers who put all of their effort into teaching. Instead, they have endless meetings to attend, they have professional development programs to attend—and those rarely provide any ideas that actually help us do the real work we do with students—they have hours and hours of paperwork, they get told to do something new every year before they finished or evaluated the results of what was done as last year's innovation. They get all of those e-mails from their department head or administrator or central office people or state department of education people telling them of some educational imperfection that must be fixed immediately. Whenever a parent or guardian or student complains about a teacher, the teachers feel that they are guilty until proven innocent. A lot of people are very frustrated.

PRINCIPAL: You know what is amazing, and for some reason I am just noticing this—we are all saying the same thing. The work our jobs require us to do is not what we expected and is not what we think is best for students. As we listen to each other, it's as if we compared notes before this meeting, but we are all up against the same difficulties and the same realities. So, what can we do about all of this?

ASSISTANT PRINCIPAL: You know what the most successful businesses do to become even more successful? They listen to customers. I took some classes to become certified to be a school district superintendent.

One great speaker in a class was the president of a big media company that owns a lot of radio stations. He said his company has to listen to their audience if they expect the radio audience to listen to their stations. They do all kinds of market research to see what radio listeners prefer. He also said that his company's chief executive officer and board of directors often give him new duties, new goals, more work. He's the president of the company, and other people tell him what to do. The same with school district superintendents. We might think that they have it made and just control their time and agenda. They take directions from the school board, the state lawmakers, plus every person in town who has a complaint thinks the superintendent should stop what she is doing and solve their problem.

SCHOOL COUNSELOR: I should have realized this before. It is so obvious. It's part of what every school counselor is taught to do. Listen. We're taught to listen. It sure sounds as if people in education need to listen to each other. I remember one article I read about a school that got great results from their LISTEN program. Actually it was not a program, it was just a way of working with people. LISTEN stands for Learning Is Strengthened Through Everyone Negotiating. My first reaction was that negotiating is for nations creating a treaty or for labor unions creating a work contract. Then I was informed that negotiating generally means that people listen to each other, people talk to each other, people communicate, people find ideas they can agree on and work together to implement. Plus negotiation means I have to really understand my perspective, my reality, and what I am up against. The other big part of good negotiating is that it does not stop. After a treaty or contract or decision is agreed to, both sides have to implement and monitor the treaty. They may have to update their original agreement based on actual results.

PRINCIPAL: How was the LISTEN program started? What got it implemented? How did it work?

SCHOOL COUNSELOR: The school I know about that uses the LISTEN idea used a long list of communication methods. Here's what I remember. Nothing was fancy or expensive or complicated. Mostly it took time and effort, but it saved time and effort by preventing some problems and by creating such a sense that everybody mattered, everyone would be listened to and taken seriously. Each day began with the school administrators, school counselors, rotating groups of teachers who took turns, and other staff members out in the halls during the half hour before school began. The adults would talk to students. There might be a topic of the day such as ask students what sport or clubs they would like to add. If there was no topic like that the conversations could be about classes, part-time jobs, grades, and other typical topics. Anything of interest would be e-mailed to the assistant principal who compiled the input each day and who would send specific comments to the person who had responsibility for that matter. Each Friday on the morning television announcements that assistant principal gave everyone a one-minute summary of the week's hallway conversations and of the follow-up status or results.

There was so much more. Once a month on different school days each school administrator and each school counselor would substitute teach for a full day. That gave them direct contact with students. When the teachers they substituted for returned to school, the administrator or counselor would discuss the classes and any related issues. At least once per semester almost every student in the school was in direct classroom contact with a school administrator or a school counselor. The bridges this built between the faculty and the school leaders were so beneficial.

What else? The principal hosted an open-microphone town hall meeting once a month after school. The assistant principal and the school counselors ate lunch in the school cafeteria at least twice per week. Students knew they were welcome to join the school leaders for lunch to discuss topics of interest.

Each faculty member was asked to send e-mail to the principal one day per week, 20 percent of the faculty on Monday, and so on. The e-mail was to include one idea to improve the school, one problem you need help with, one complaint/suggestion, and one success story or other good news. Responses or follow-up would occur soon.

Students, faculty, and staff could offer a thirty-second video editorial on the morning television news. Classrooms were absolutely silent during these presentations.

I'm sure there were other parts to the LISTEN program, but those I mentioned stand out. The best part was that the school saw a large reduction in discipline referrals, a reduction in suspensions from school, an increase in attendance by the students and teachers. There was also a higher number of students on the honor roll.

Oh, in the second year of LISTEN, the school invited the school board members to be in the halls for that thirty-minute period before school whenever they would. Central office personnel were invited to substitute teach or to eat lunch at school. What surprised everyone was how many teachers started eating lunch in the cafeteria so they could talk to the central office staff. Some great ideas and partnerships got started with more lunch visits. The central office workers said they usually had to go to some restaurant for lunch so why not go to school cafeterias and get a good meal at a bargain price while doing some face-to-face work that they otherwise might never find the time to get done.

PRINCIPAL: It's getting late and I know that everyone has places to go. Take a few days, please, and think about this LISTEN idea. Talk to me or e-mail me in the next few days to let me know what you think we should do about listening at this school, or let me know if you think no action is needed. Thanks for your time and your ideas today. It was good to get everyone together to talk and to listen.

Leadership and management require more than listening, but if listening is excluded from leadership and management the results will be limited, at best, and turbulent, at worst. Leaders and managers in the education universe are very busy people who have many demands on their time and on their skills. Continually increasing demands are one reason why listening needs to be increased.

No governor, no state legislator, no state commissioner of education, no school district superintendent, no school board member, no school administrator has time to waste. That also means there is no time to spend on actions that do not solve the real problems in schools. What is the most efficient way to identify the real strengths of a school, the real problems at a school, and the real priorities that should be dealt with at a school? Ask the teachers at that school to tell you what the strengths are, what the problems are, and what the priorities should be.

In a democracy other input should also be encouraged. Taxpayers, parents, guardians, students, interest groups, civic or community groups, local businesses should be heard; however, their perspective does not include the classroom reality information that only teachers know because only teachers are in classrooms all day, every day.

It is far too common for a national television network to broadcast a news story about a school in Idaho that implemented a new reading program with favorable results. The local school district expanded the program. The political leaders in that state decided that every school in the state should use this new program. People across the nation saw the news report and began asking why the program was not being used at their local schools. By the time schools in other states implemented the program, the original Idaho school became concerned that their initial achievement gains were not being sustained; in fact, reading progress was replaced by reading scores going down. The original Idaho school abandoned the program while some people in other states began implementing the program. One size of a solution does not fit all sizes of all problems. Educational trends are to be evaluated with a high degree of serious inquiry. The warning label should state, "Do not try this solution at your school until you are certain of the real problems at your school and until you are certain that this is the best solution for those real problems."

The history of education reform in the United States is a series of one reform being replaced by the next reform. Perhaps this shows a commendable persistence that confirms a national, state, and local determination to identify the ultimate education reform that once and for all will get the desired student achievement results. Perhaps this is a misguided search for magical wonders that do not exist. Do not be discouraged. Finding the right solution requires looking in the right place.

If my doctor hears my description of throat pain, dryness, or irritation what will he do? He will look in my throat. He will check some other factors, but since the problem involved my throat, he will look at my throat.

Where does education happen? In classrooms. Where do we need to look to identify what is working well in education or what needs to be improved? In classrooms. Who do we need to listen to in order to identify the current reality in classrooms? Teachers. That is logical, feasible, practical, and sensible. That also requires no new laws, regulations, policies, or taxes. Massive reforms do require new laws, regulations, policies, and taxes. Reform after reform after reform can get very frustrating, expensive, and counterproductive. That is the topic of the next chapter.

THE FRUSTRATIONS OF REFORM AFTER REFORM AFTER REFORM

From a teacher's perspective it can easily seem as if the president, congress, governors, state legislators, school board members, some school superintendents, and some school principals are seeking to find and to implement the ultimate systemic, structural, bureaucratic, political, organizational, managerial, regulated reform of education. The goals of this ultimate reform could be that no student will be left "unsmart," unhealthy, or unsuccessful.

That flawless structural reform of education does not exist and will never exist. Some systems, structures, organization charts, laws, policies, regulations impacting education are superior to others; however, the most important goal in education—to cause learning—is not a function of systems, structures, organization charts, laws, policies, or regulations as much as it is what teachers and students do in classrooms.

To acknowledge the limits of, if not the futility of, some structural reform of education is not an admission of unavoidable failure, but rather it is a liberating realization that chasing the next reform dream/illusion will result in yet another frustration, while concentrating relentlessly on what matters most—what teachers and students do in classrooms—can bring outstanding results.

If political leaders, community leaders, interest group members, national or state education officials, or school board members were asked what concerns them most about schools and students, and then were asked what encourages them most about schools and students, what answers would be expected? Take those expected answers and compare/contrast them with answers that teachers provided in the research survey for this book. What do you expect the teachers will say? Let's see how close your predictions are to the exact comments. "What concerns you most about schools today?"

- "We are not preparing students for the demands of the work world where deadlines and standards don't change. We say we care about kids, but we really only care about their test scores."
- "Lack of respect for teachers from both parents and students."
- "Lack of discipline. Also, the large amounts of assessments required."
- "Emphasis on tests instead of learning."
- "Schools do not have many consequences that can be imposed as discipline actions. I'm also concerned about safety."
- "Passing students on with minimum passing grades but without real academic preparation."
- "Too much to do in too little time."
- "Society."
- "What concerns me the most is student mental health. I see lots of students who are hurting deeply. They abuse substances, cut themselves, engage in antisocial behavior, and reject norms of acceptable behavior. Where are the parents of these kids?"
- "The burnout that teachers feel and how many people leave teaching."

"What encourages you most about schools today?"

- "The fact that despite it all, we persevere and continue to work with our students."
- "They are places for kids to be safe, get fed, and have other needs met for at least six hours of their day."
- "I see many teachers who care and who sacrifice daily for the good of kids. The rest of society should be very, very grateful. God knows

what many of these kids could be capable of doing that is bad, but some teacher came along and warmed their heart. Maybe the impact on that one kid is slight, but I tell you in all seriousness, it's holding our society together."
- "Students."
- "Schools are always trying to get better."
- "Coming together of faculty and staff to help one another."
- Our schools have some exciting programs for our kids that allow them to showcase their interests and talents."
- "We haven't lost our sense of humor yet."
- "We have more resources than ever before. We offer opportunities for success to everyone."

What overall ideas and themes run through the concerns about schools that teachers expressed? What overall ideas and themes run through the aspect of schools that encourages teachers? Does the word "people" apply to both questions as we look for an overall idea or theme? Teachers are concerned about students. Teachers know that students are real people living real lives right now so those concerns are reality. Teachers are encouraged by people who achieve, who work, who try, who help, who make a difference.

The very best laws, policies, regulations, systems, leadership methods, and managerial styles can be helpful, but those actions can be superficial, bureaucratic, or distant. Teachers who responded to this book's survey as shown in the samples above remind us that what is done to directly impact people in helpful ways is what matters most. In schools that means teachers and students in classrooms must be the emphasis for, the reason for everything that is done. With proper emphasis on students emerging from the questions about schools, we now get more specific.

"What concerns you most about students today?"

- "Some are being trained to believe that nothing is their fault and someone will always save them."
- "The increase of apathy."
- "The large amount of apathy—I have five students not graduating, and they don't seem to care."
- "So many have little or no respect for authority."

- "Disrespect and lack of motivation."
- "Some do not have guidance at home. Many lack morals and values. Consequences mean nothing to them. The bad kids are the cool kids at school."
- "Lack of personal responsibility. Parents will always do, fix, or rescue."
- "My greatest concern is how rapidly society is changing. I wonder, will some of these kids who are not progressing become productive citizens, or will they hold the rest of us back and become a drain on society. How will these kids be able to compete in the global economy that is becoming more and more competitive?"
- "They don't know how to make good decisions. The awful role models they follow from society. They have no idea how disrespectful they can be and the consequences that will come because of it."
- "The lack of personal responsibility they take for their education. The sense of entitlement they have."

"What encourages you most about students today?"

- "I see them learning every single day."
- "They do want to do well."
- "When you reach them, they amaze you!"
- "More and more kids have the goal of going to college."
- "The students who have respect, great work ethic, self-pride, and motivation. Students who work hard for themselves."
- "The majority are excited about learning and want to learn."
- "Many of our students are active members of their churches or other community groups. That gives me hope because they do seem to want to help others in need."
  - "Some are eager, thoughtful, and enthusiastic."

Based on the survey responses dealing with concerns about schools and students plus encouraging thoughts about schools and students, consider the next two case studies. Which case study is consistent with the survey responses? Which is inconsistent? What explains the use of two such different approaches?

CASE STUDY 3.1

PRINCIPAL: I am just going to be blunt and honest. We have to do this. I know you are busy. I know this is not what you asked for or what you need. Still, it is required. We don't have a choice. Every school in our school district is doing this same six-hour professional development training. Mostly it involves watching three hours of video materials. Then, working in small groups for three hours, you discuss the videos and you plan ways that you will include this new set of reading strategies in your lessons. What questions do you have so far?

MATH TEACHER: Why in the world are we doing anything like this again? The school year begins in less than a week. Every teacher at our high school has too much to do and not enough time to do it. So we spend six hours today on some system of teaching reading skills or improving reading skills. Sure, we have some students who still struggle with reading, and we have some students who read the most complex material known to mankind. This sounds like one more government mandate that allows the president or the governor to proclaim how serious our society is about every student being an outstanding reader.

SCIENCE TEACHER: I read about this program in some education journals. The research basis for the program is not very strong. The program's marketing seems better than its actual content. The program is called WORD, which stands for Wonderful Outstanding Reading Development. There is nothing new or amazing about this program. We could probably create a better reading program ourselves, but the education powers that be don't trust us to do that.

HISTORY TEACHER: Is it correct to think that there must be some money involved? The rumor is that each school that completes the training gets $2,500, all from the federal government, and the school district gets a matching $2,500 per school. Then at the end of the school year if you can show that the WORD program was implemented, your school gets another $2,500, and so does your school district. So for our school to get $5,000 we are forced to go through this six-hour training today, implement this program, and then fill out a form in May to explain how we implemented the WORD program. One hundred twenty-five teachers have to go through all of that so the school gets $5,000 and so the school district gets $5,000. If we donated or raised $40 per teacher, it would add up to $5,000. Do we have that option?

PRINCIPAL: No. Like I said, we have no options. The U.S. Congress passed a national reading improvement act that the president signed into law. The U.S. Department of Education wrote the regulations telling the states how to implement the law. Our state's department of education and our state's board of education did their part to show every school district how to enforce this law throughout the state. Our school district leaders and our school board approved the plan that we are following. We don't have the time, the resources, or the option of challenging everyone from the president to the local school board. We just have to do this.

ENGLISH TEACHER: I've taught English at this high school for twenty-nine years. I've seen programs like WORD come and go. I've seen the national government and the state government get all worked up every five to ten years. Every time a president or a governor or some gathering of business executives proclaims that students are not reading as well as students in some other country, we end up with some knee-jerk reading program to implement. The only good news is that these programs never last. This will be a one-year fizzle, and then it will be over. Everyone up the chain of command will be able to tell their boss or their constituents how thoroughly the WORD program was implemented. I'd suggest that we get started so we can get the training over with and then we can get some real work done to get ready for the first day of school.

PRINCIPAL: Good idea. The video material is divided into four parts, and each is forty-five minutes long. It's 8:40 now, so with a break or two we'll finish the videos by noon. Lunch is provided today so we'll eat at noon. You'll work in small groups from 12:30 to 3:30. The groups will be by department so you'll get to work with the other teachers in your subject area. At 3:30 each department head will give me the required written summary of your department's action plan to use the WORD program in your classes throughout the year. OK, here's the first video segment, WORD—Wonderful Outstanding Reading Development: How to make WORD the best friend of each teacher.

As the video began, one teacher was commenting to a colleague, "This school district has twenty schools. Twenty times $5,000 means the school district could get $100,000 for every school doing this. I don't know much about the WORD program, but I can think of some choice words to describe this whole process."

The other teacher replied, "$5,000 per school for the school, $5,000 more per school to the school district. There are 1,700 schools in this state—$10,000 times 1,700 is $17 million. Imagine all of the better ways that money could be used. Imagine the better ways our time could be used. We're getting paid for this day to watch these videos. I bet this day will cost $25,000 to cover every teacher and principal for one day's pay. Makes the $5,000 the school will get look pretty small."

CASE STUDY 3.2

PRINCIPAL: Thanks to everyone for being on time. It's May 6, and this is a very busy time in the school year, so let's get to the agenda of this faculty meeting. The first topic is a request for input. As you know, our reading scores have improved in recent years, but the school district is concerned that in many schools across the district reading scores are stable or are showing limited progress. Our improvement in reading showed less increase last year than the year before, so we need to think about this. The district leaders have made it clear to each principal that they realize one size does not fit all. No one reading program or effort will work in every school because the needs, the students, the reading status of each school is different. So, please take the next three minutes and at your tables discuss ideas for how our school could better develop the reading skills of each individual student. Then we'll listen to the ideas you identify.

The conversations at the tables are rather lively. At least two or three teachers at each table are asking important questions or offering valid ideas. Sure, a few people are not fully attentive or are having a social conversation, but the overall level of concentration and involvement is strong.

PRINCIPAL: Good work. You noticed that as you were talking, the assistant principals, counselors, and I brought snacks to each table. Please help yourself to those goodies. Those of you who have a May birthday have a little birthday cake that our dean of students made and just brought to you. So, birthday people, please stand up and we'll cheer for you. Now, let's trade ideas about reading. Good, Mr. Jacobs, you start for us, and then everyone else with an idea, please join in.

"Time. The issue is always time. Do we take time to specifically teach reading? Do we try to teach reading as we are also teaching our subject? Our conversation was about the concern that the school schedule really does not have any room to add new instructional programs. If we begin to teach reading skills in every class we have to give up something in each class."

"Our group thought that since so many teachers are taking graduate school classes, if their classes include any ideas about how to make students better readers, those teachers could share that with all of us. It is common for some teachers to take extra graduate classes in the summer, so in August before school starts we could hear from our colleagues who learned good reading ideas at graduate school classes or at conferences and workshops attended during the summer."

"Our idea is similar to that because it applies the knowledge of this faculty. Some teachers here know more about how to teach reading than other teachers do. Let's schedule a time when our most effective reading teachers can tell everyone exactly what they are doing in their classrooms to get good results. We have success stories right here, but we rarely get to visit other classrooms. So let's share the success stories in a meeting in August."

"Great idea. Our group endorsed the share-good-ideas plan. We thought that the school could set up a place on the school's electronic bulletin board for teachers where examples of lesson plans and classroom activities that include effective reading instruction could be posted for everyone to see. We get a lot of information on that electronic bulletin board, so let's add good reading methods."

"Our group talked about books. Some teachers have used the assignment where students create a magazine about a topic that relates to the class. The student in physics class who made the magnificent magazine about roller coasters was an example. We thought of a semester project for juniors or seniors to create a book. The students complain about all of the writing pieces they have to create for their senior year writing collection. Maybe if they could create a book that is about an academic topic and that includes the different types of writing their senior collection must have, it would mean more to them. A book about roller coasters could include everything from analysis of data to fictional considerations of the roller coaster of the future."

"Several of us in our group were concerned about ninth graders and tenth graders who are barely literate. We might need some very targeted help for those students. We even wondered if their schedules could include two or three hours daily in a reading class that included English and social studies so they keep on schedule with credits for graduation, but so they get caught up in reading."

"We agree. We even wondered if the school district could have a reading program connected with the vocational program. Take ninth graders who barely read and put them in a vocational reading program. They read as they learn to repair cars or design websites or do television broadcasting. Connect reading to some other activity that intrigues them and their commitment could be very impressive."

PRINCIPAL: Great thinking. Any other ideas? Not now, OK, but let's give ourselves the rest of the week to think about this. I'll e-mail everyone a summary of the ideas that were presented today. We've worked on reading before, but today's students are different from yesterday's students. What worked a few years ago may not work now or may need some adjustment. Then, again, an old idea might deserve to be tried again—maybe it was discarded too soon. Before this school year ends we will set some goals for reading instruction and reading results for next year. We will also agree on the best way for every teacher to learn about the most effective instructional methods to improve reading skills in our students.

We have one other topic on the agenda. There are some awards you will vote on for seniors. So, our senior class sponsor, Mr. Buckner, will lead us on that.

What differences are most obvious and are most significant in the approaches taken in the two case studies? Which approach applies the knowledge, insight, and perception of teachers? Which approach is consistent with Dr. Earl Reum's aphorism "People support what they help create"? Which approach is more likely to build commitment from people at the school level? Which approach is more likely to actually have a favorable impact on reading skills of students?

What causes situations such as the bureaucratic mandate shown in the first case study? Perhaps a school declines year after year as evaluated by some testing system and the national, state, or local government imposes correction plans, sanctions, or other actions. Perhaps legal action has been brought against a school district and rapid responses must occur with no time for input. Those two circumstances apply to a minority of schools and do not necessitate a national or state requirement of identical actions being imposed on all schools.

What creates the circumstances where a school uses the method, or a similar method, of the second case study? Perhaps an enlightened school principal leads and manages the school in a very participatory way so the decision-making process is shared and so input is sincerely sought. Perhaps a school district superintendent promised herself that her work as an educational administrator would always be done with the heart and soul of a teacher so she always expects of herself and of her administration in the district an aggressive pursuit of input from faculty and staff. Perhaps a principal kept a list of promises while he was a teacher and then while he was an assistant principal. The list was of promises he made to himself about how he would do the job of principal when he was given that opportunity to lead and manage a school.

Classrooms, not bureaucracies, are the places where education happens. The only people in the education universe who work directly with students all day, every day are teachers. The best possible school improvement cannot occur without direct, comprehensive input from teachers. Teachers deal with the classroom realities all day, every day. Education reforms that work must impact and must improve the classroom reality. National consulting firms and statewide interest groups have not been in the classrooms they seek to impact as much as teachers have. Why let people who—despite good intentions and despite an abundance of data presented in Hollywood motion picture artistic style—do not know the reality of your school, your school district, or your state play major roles in shaping the educational improvement plans for your school, your school district, or your state?

Among the strongest and the most discouraging frustrations teachers have mentioned to me through the past three decades is their resentment of the annual proclamation by an educational administrator at the state, school district, or school level of "this year's new way of teaching." Last year's new way of teaching was not fully implemented or evaluated. What happened to it? A new commissioner of education for the state, a new governor, a new school district superintendent, a new principal, or a new law requires some new program for the year. Governors, commissioners, superintendents, principals, laws come, go, come back, go again, and each one could bring new mandates for teachers to use in classrooms. Despite the frustrations of enduring another one-year wonder to implement in August and to replace next August, most teachers stand the test of time. Many versions of "this year's new way of teaching" fail the test of time because they fail the classroom reality test.

What do students remember about the academic, the instructional, the classroom part of school? Textbooks? No. A new requirement from the state department of education? Double no. Students remember teachers who cared, who made learning real, who took a personal interest, who insisted that you did your best work, who liked teaching, who liked students, who showed up at the events in the school or in the community that students were involved in, who listened, who exemplified the work ethic students were expected to demonstrate, who never gave up on a student, who challenged students, who used a variety of teaching methods, who were enthusiastic, and who connected the students' wholesome knowledge, talents, and interests with the material to be learned at school.

Multiple research projects done by graduate students of mine for about ten years confirm the conclusions in the above paragraph. My research results involving more than four thousand people over a ten-year span confirm the same conclusions. When graduates recall what mattered most to them in their kindergarten through high school experience, they think of their best teachers. They do not think of laws, policies, regulations, bureaucracies, or reforms although those, if done well, are needed. They think of their best teachers because it is those teachers who touch the lives of those students. For any education reform to actually improve what happens in schools, the reality of what matters most in schools—what teachers and students do in classrooms—must be the decisive factor.

CASE STUDY 3.3

GOVERNOR: We have to do something. Every newspaper editorial is critical about the educational system in this state. I know that everyone in the schools says how hard they work and how difficult their job is, but in the campaign I promised to be the education governor, and with the national rankings still showing our state ranked forty-third or forty-fourth in education categories, I'll have some tough questions to answer when I run for another term. So, what should we do?

SPEAKER OF THE STATE HOUSE OF REPRESENTATIVES: Every conference we attend has session after session about education. When the governors from across the nation meet, education is a major topic. When state legislators from our region or from the nation meet, the topics are education and economic development and the rising costs of pensions. I've heard some good ideas at these conferences. Can we borrow what is working in other states and use those ideas here?

LIEUTENANT GOVERNOR: I met last month with the state association of school superintendents. I met last week with the state association of school principals. They are not asking for any major actions from us. In fact, they said that the changes our administration proposed and got approved two years ago are just getting implemented now. They can't tell yet what results will come from those changes. What we did two years ago was a collection of ideas that had worked in other states. You remember what our political consultants told us about the results other candidates in other states got when their campaigns used the same ideas we used. The election results showed that those campaign ideas worked in the campaigns of six out of seven states where our professional political consultants managed what a candidate for governor said in the campaign.

GOVERNOR: I know that those educational reform ideas came from campaigns in other states. I know that more reform ideas were associated with victorious candidates including us. We won the election three years ago. We got an education reform package approved by the legislature two years ago. Finally those reforms are getting put into action, but there are no results yet, no improvements. People are lining up to run against me, and newspaper editorials are critical. Other candidates will be critical. I promised education reform. I promised results. So, what do we do now to get some fast results?

ASSISTANT TO THE GOVERNOR: You have earned some very positive press coverage about the task forces you established on the environment, on alternative energy sources, on reforming state employee pension plans, and on more use of technology in state government. What happens if you appoint a task force of highly respected people from all over the state to study education? They can provide a report to you next year just in time for you to include their recommendations as part of your re-election campaign.

GOVERNOR: Give that some thought. Come up with a long list of people who could be on that task force. Be sure every possible interest group, civic group, demographic group, labor union, education group, and others are included. Think about how we justify another task force on education. Every governor in recent memory has done a task force on education. Think about how we explain that what we did two years ago needs a task force to review those reforms and to make new recommendations. Are we missing anything?

PRESS SECRETARY: We haven't said much about educators. We mentioned the superintendents and principals, but what about teachers. Don't we need their input? Can we include teachers on the task force?

LIEUTENANT GOVERNOR: Of course, include a few, but not too many. I have not heard from many teachers, but my guess is that they just want more money, money, money.

PRESS SECRETARY: Has anyone here visited a school recently? The governor went to a few schools two years ago to introduce reform ideas and then to sign the school reform bill into law. Has anyone here actually been in a school lately? It would be a great photo opportunity.

GOVERNOR: Who has time to go to schools? We have to fix the education problems, not go look at the education problems. Let's meet in one week to review the task force details. Keep this discussion to yourselves. We don't need any information leaks to the press while we are just developing our plan.

The governor's task force on education innovation, reform, and results was approved as the way to lead this state from the bottom part of all national rankings about education toward the top of those rankings. The task force divided its one hundred members into ten committees to study the ten different topics listed below.

1. Early childhood education.
2. Funding for education.
3. Elementary schools.
4. Middle schools.

5. High schools
6. Transitions.
   a. Elementary to middle school
   b. Middle school to high school
   c. High school to work, military, higher education, technical or vocational training
7. Parent, guardian, community involvement in schools.
8. School safety and security.
9. Teacher preparation programs in colleges and universities.
10. Curriculum and instruction.

The task force held many meetings. The ten committees held many meetings, some in the state capital and others in every part of the state. Each committee had a website with easy methods for citizen input. Educators were invited via e-mail to attend meetings.

The task force completed its work and presented the governor with a 225-page report about education. The report was called SCHOOL, which stood for Students Can Have Outstanding Opportunities for Learning. The governor promised that his second term in office would be dedicated to full implementation of the ideas in the SCHOOL report. The governor was not re-elected for a second term.

There were many reasons that the governor was defeated in his re-election effort. His opponent repeatedly asked, "Are our schools better than they were four years ago?" Crowds would yell "No!" whenever he asked the question. The opponent also criticized the governor for taking the time to create the SCHOOL report saying, "We do not need a school report. We need school action. I'll be the governor who takes action on education." Whether the new governor can get better, faster results will depend on many factors, none more important than addressing the classroom reality that is of concern to many people in concept, but that is known best by teachers through direct, daily personal experience.

CASE STUDY 3.4

The school district's superintendent had announced in January that she would retire at the end of June when her current three-year contract ended. After thirty-two years in education she had decided to stay in this profession as a part-time college instructor. The school district's school board hired a professional executive search firm to help seek candidates and to help screen candidates. The $55,000 fee for the search firm inspired several critical letters to the editor along with frustrated conversations during lunch in faculty lounges, but the decision had been made, and there would be no reversal of the decision. Still, some teachers wondered if the school district's human resources department does a good job with the employment process for all of the other employees in the school district, why not have that department search for superintendent candidates so the $55,000 could be saved.

The school board and the school district hosted four community input sessions and two school district employee input sessions. The intention was to identify the most important traits, experiences, ideas that the ideal new superintendent would bring to the job. As can often happen, the ideal new superintendent would resemble a superhero more than a human being, but there would be no harm in thinking big.

Eventually there were three finalists for the position of superintendent. These experienced, knowledgeable, qualified finalists attended a public forum and for one hour answered questions from the audience. The opening statements, answers to three questions, and closing statements are below. In terms of listening to teachers and in terms of emphasizing actions that truly benefit the classroom reality, how would you rank these three finalists?

OPENING STATEMENT:

MR. ADAMS: It is a pleasure to be in Newtown today. Everything I know about your community is very impressive. Everything I have seen during my visits here has been impressive. I am eager to answer your questions, to get acquainted, and to work with you.

MS. JEFFERSON: As you know, I have lived in Newtown all my life. I have attended school here. I have worked in this school district for twenty-nine years. I could retire, but there is more to do and, to be blunt, only someone who has known this community for decades can provide the type of trusted personal touch that our school district needs. I have been a teacher, assistant principal, principal, curriculum specialist, and assistant superintendent. I can do the superintendent job on the first day. You know me, and I know you. Let's get to work.

DR. FRANKLIN: Few jobs are more demanding in this nation than to be the superintendent of an urban school district. My résumé shows that I have served as superintendent in four large cities. Also, I have been one state's assistant commissioner of education, and I have worked for the U.S. Department of Education. Through those experiences I have become aware of what works best in schools throughout our country. I bring to Newtown a plan for education reform that has worked elsewhere and that can work here if I am given the opportunity to show you the plan and to use the plan in Newtown.

FIRST QUESTION: Newtown School District's overall test scores have changed very little in the past two years. The state government and the national government expect improvement. What would you do to get our test scores up?

MR. ADAMS: My current job is associate director of testing programs and analysis for our state's department of education. I have analyzed Newtown's testing data. There are a few areas of recent progress, but there are many areas of real concern. I've worked in the testing and measurement field for almost twenty years. I've taught graduate school classes on these topics. In the past four years I have spoken to twenty-five professional groups about issues related to test scores. I know the tests, I know the best test-taking strategies, and I know what has worked in other similar school districts to get test scores up. Like it or not, the state government and the national government concentrate on these test scores. This is an area where I can do Newtown a lot of good.

MS. JEFFERSON: Tests, tests, tests. We are obsessed with tests. If all you want are higher test scores, then select someone else. I'm sure that we can find ways to improve our test scores, but not by living in fear of the test scores. Have you talked to any students or to any teachers about the annual tests the state requires? I have talked to them. I hear their frustrations with tests, tests, and more tests. The answer to our test scores is not found by narrowly emphasizing test scores. The answer is found in schools, in classrooms, in curriculum, in instruction. If we do everything positive to get great teaching and great learning in every classroom, the improved test scores will follow.

DR. FRANKLIN: I've been a superintendent. I know how important test scores are. I know that each school has test scores they have to reach and that the school district overall has a comprehensive test score to reach. My record shows that in each district where I have been superintendent I brought a proven test score improvement plan that each board of education approved and that every school in each district was required to use. Sure, some people complained, but we were able to show improvement or to stop decline in test scores. To get test scores up in Newtown, I am confident that the plan I have used in other school districts can work here.

SECOND QUESTION: What ideas do you have to improve the professional development program for teachers?

MR. ADAMS: Before I became our state's associate director of testing programs and analysis, I worked as our state's interim assistant director for professional development and teacher certification. I have attended many conferences about professional development. I have served on the national task force that evaluated professional development programs. I have published several articles about effective professional development in state and national education journals. I wrote a chapter for a book about professional development. That book was edited by a national expert in professional development. So, I bring a vast range of information about professional development.

MS. JEFFERSON: I'll be blunt. Most of the professional development programs, conferences, workshops, and meetings I have attended or that I am aware of accomplish very little. To be honest, from what teachers tell me, most of the professional development sessions they are required to attend never really deal with what the teachers need to know. The professional development that is best for teachers deals with the real issues and problems that teachers face. Why do we keep sending teachers to expensive conferences in San Diego in February? Why do we keep paying thousands of dollars to have expensive guest speakers come to our school district, put on their very scripted show, take our money, and leave us with our problems? Here's what I recommend. Ask teachers what they need to learn about and then provide professional development on those topics. Also, put the skills of our people to use. Teachers can teach other teachers. One teacher needs ideas about getting students interested in writing so we match that teacher with someone in the same school who has been very successful in getting students excited about writing. Teachers hate professional development for the same reason so many students hate some classes—the topics just don't relate to them. We can fix some of those problems. How do I know that? There are schools right here in Newtown with good professional development that teachers appreciate. Maybe it is like some of the students say—you just have to make it real.

DR. FRANKLIN: I've studied this topic very thoroughly. In my duties as a school district superintendent I always made professional development a high priority for school administrators and for teachers. I have always insisted that schools make a five-year professional development plan so the professional development had some continuity. Far too often the professional development training in one year has nothing to do with the PD of the prior year. People feel pushed and pulled when every school year has a totally new PD emphasis. Some national experts I have worked with created some curriculum materials for schools to use for a five-year PD plan that has continuity built in. I would ask our schools in Newtown to use more very good materials that I have seen work in other school districts.

THIRD QUESTION: The highest priority of any school district is student achievement. Explain to us what you will do to improve student achievement in this school district.

MR. ADAMS: The research we have done in the state's Office of Testing Programs and Analysis shows what the most successful school districts in the state have done to increase student achievement as measured by the annual state tests. First, every teacher knows exactly what the state has said that students are supposed to learn. Successful schools confirm that whether you teach twelfth-grade physics or fourth-grade reading you know the exact curriculum content that your students are supposed to master. Second, the teachers emphasize the exact curriculum content. Day after day, the successful schools put the emphasis on the curriculum that will be tested. Third, successful schools spend time during the school year giving tests that are very similar to the annual state tests in format, in topics included, and in length. My experience analyzing school after school shows how effective that three-part plan can be.

THE FRUSTRATIONS OF REFORM AFTER REFORM 57

Ms. Jefferson: I would keep doing what I have been doing in this school district for the past twenty-nine years. There was never any problem in my classroom with student achievement. My students learned. My students achieved. Every job I have done since I left the classroom has been done with the awareness that my job was to help teachers and students do their job. I do not bring some package of materials that came out of some education supply catalog. I do not bring some plan that the national education journals recommend. I also do not bring ten or twenty initiatives, each one directed at some tiny group within the school district. I bring a conviction that if people who are getting great results with students can share their success stories with people who are not getting great results, there would be many benefits. We don't need to spend a fortune on new materials, new systems, or new training. We just need to be sure that effective teaching occurs each day in each classroom. Then everyone wins.

Dr. Franklin: The student achievement question is being asked all over the country. In every school district where I have served as superintendent, we got good results with a system called STRETCH, which stands for Students and Teachers Results Enhanced Through Curriculum Harmony. The program takes the school district's entire curriculum from kindergarten through the senior year of high school and shows teachers for each subject and each grade level exactly what curriculum content is to be worked on each week. This system eliminates any doubt about what is done week to week, year to year, grade to grade. This system also meant that every teacher throughout the school district knew what was expected. Parents and guardians like the precise predictability of the program. I'm convinced that for every problem in education a tested, developed, ready-to-be-used program exists.

Closing Statement:

Dr. Franklin: We could talk for hours, but it is time to conclude. Thank you, citizens and educators of Newtown for being here today and for including me in this public forum. My record stands for itself. I am ready, willing, and able to be your superintendent. I have been a superintendent so I know the job. I know what actions have worked in other school districts, and I will bring more actions, plans, programs, and ideas with me. If you are looking for someone to come here with experience, ability, and solutions to your problems, I am the person you are looking for.

Ms. Jefferson: I know what some of you are thinking, so I'll say it for you—we cannot select someone from our school district because that person has friends to take care of and enemies who will never cooperate. Let's think differently. I know the Newtown school district. I know you, the people of Newtown. I know the new ideas in education, and I know the old ideas in education. I read about what other schools and what other school districts all over the state and the nation are doing. I'm much more impressed with what Newtown's best schools, best teachers, best students are doing. I'd like to be the superintendent who is of, by, and for Newtown, who connects local problems with proven local solutions. We can make that happen. I ask for the opportunity to do that with you.

Mr. Adams: The constitution of our state makes it clear that education is a duty of the state government. Of course, the state works through and with local school districts to get the job done in each local community. My experience with our state's department of education is a very important strength to bring. Schools and school districts have to know what the state requires and have to comply with all state mandates. I know the state government's laws, policies, and regulations about education. I know the state testing plan. Any school district that is serious about improving education needs to be led by someone who knows the political realities of state government, someone who is known by the state's political leaders and education leaders, someone who can help us navigate every storm the bureaucracy sends our way. I bring those unique skills to Newtown. I hope that we will begin working together soon.

Who will the school board select to be the new superintendent? There would be months involved in the overall process of seeking applications, reviewing applications, working with the professional search firm, getting community input about important skills and characteristics, narrowing the applicant pool, having initial interviews, checking many references, conducting a second round of interviews, having a public forum for the finalists—perhaps appearing together or maybe appearing individually—and then making a final decision.

What differences are most obvious between Mr. Adams, Ms. Jefferson, and Dr. Franklin? Which of the three finalists is more in touch with the importance of listening to teachers so the classroom reality that teachers uniquely know can be part of every decision that impacts teachers', students', classrooms' work? Will the school board insist that someone from outside the school district must be brought in so they can bring with them the school reforms, plans, programs, and systems that travel throughout the country via the circuit of conventions, conferences, workshops, professional development programs, and people who change jobs from school district to school district or from state to state? There are times when a school district must select someone from another city or another state to fill a vacant executive position; however, beware of the résumé-builder or the nomad who would stay for a short time, accomplish a limited amount, and take the next good offer. When it is possible to promote from within, that provides some useful continuity, and it shows other people in the school district that their career goals could be reached without going elsewhere.

Teachers become frustrated by a series of reforms, each one lasting only a short time. Teachers become frustrated by similarly rapid change in the local school district superintendency, school board membership, state education department executives, and governors. One reason for the frustration is the perception of teachers that each new person in one of these positions brings a different school reform program that is to be implemented now. What is to be done with the last school reform program that was said to be the most significant improvement plan for schools in the past century?

Teachers have to do what they are told to do by laws, policies, regulations, school administrators, and other official power brokers in the education universe. There is continuous change—some useful, some pointless, some effective, some wasteful, some helpful, some destructive—in laws, policies, regulations, and the political power structure in the education universe. Three fundamental certainties in the education universe are students, teachers, and classrooms. Concentrating on the realities faced by students and teachers in the classroom could reduce the frequency of school reform while also increasing the meaningful results achieved through school reform.

When education reform efforts include abundant input from direct educators—teachers—the reform benefits from being based on reality. Yes, a few teachers will complain, will ask for more pay and insist on less work. That is not the input that will be applied to serious, realistic education reform. The research for this book shows ideas from and commitments from teachers who are eagerly working with students, who are enduring the difficulties, who are determined to get results, and who have some very practical, genuine, honest concerns that education reform and education reformers must hear, take seriously, and make every effort to act upon.

When education reform efforts are based mostly on input from managerial educators, organizational educators, education influentials, and social reformers, the reform can emphasize the extremities, the organization chart, the systems, the procedures, and the bureaucracy of the education universe instead of directly touching the heart, soul, and mind of the education universe. You get one chance to answer these questions: (1) where is the heart, soul, and mind of the education universe, and (2) who do you find in the heart, soul, and mind of the education universe? The answers are (1) the classroom, and (2) teachers and students.

Education reform will continue. To our society's credit, effort is made continuously to improve schools through various reform efforts, plans, programs, or laws. A court could order education reform. A governor and the state legislature could initiate education reform. Interest groups, community groups, political groups, the media could apply political pressure for educational reform. School boards can approve education improvement plans. Principals can work to reform their school. Teachers who know that education reform will continue during and after their careers are teachers who realize that the history of education reform after reform will continue.

Reform in education is a given, a fact, a certainty, a continuum. Failed reform is unnecessary but is too common. Reform success can become more likely—in truth, highly likely, if the reform has a foundation of reality. The most important reality in the education universe is the classroom. For education reform to work at the best possible level of success, the fundamental basis of the reform must be a clear, complete understanding of the classroom reality. What do teachers know about education that no other person knows? Teachers know today's classroom reality. Education reformers, please, listen to teachers. Teachers, with all the authority you have within the limits of law, policies, regulations, reform your classroom day after day to constantly improve the educational experience your students have and the career experience you have.

The education universe must revolve around the classroom. The classroom must not be required to revolve around the educational bureaucracy, network of laws, organization charts, political powers, or social reformers. Scientific, cultural, sociological, and other thinking changed when people accepted that the earth revolves around the sun. Agreeing that the classroom is the center of the education universe could be similarly enlightening, emancipating, and efficient.

The most sensitive, wise, and willing-to-listen education reformers, managerial educators, organizational educators, education influentials, and social reformers still are not in classrooms all day, every day as teachers are. There is a divide that different jobs impose. The next two chapters explore that divide.

4

THE PARTIAL DIVIDE

A principal or an assistant principal always has to respond to the unexpected, the unscheduled, the unusual, and the daily to-do list. Phone calls, e-mails, parents or guardians who show up at school insisting that they must see the principal immediately, problems in the building or on the campus grounds, personnel matters, interviews, hiring new staff, budgets, discipline referrals, requests, complaints, meetings, reports to submit, forms to fill out, fire drills, severe weather drills, earthquake drills, school lockdown drills, power outages, late buses, substitute teachers for whom no lesson plan was left, vandalism to the building, mechanical or structural problems with the building, mandates from the central office, media inquiries, plus there is instructional leadership.

While principals and assistant principals complete the duties listed above and more, teachers are in their classrooms with students. School-level administrators and teachers work in the same building but have vastly different duties. Those vastly different duties mean that teachers and principals/assistant principals typically spend very little time together and spend very little time working together on the same project.

While an assistant principal searches the building or the campus grounds for a student who was vulgar to a teacher, ran out of the classroom, slammed the classroom door, and was last seen running toward an

THE PARTIAL DIVIDE

exit, teachers are in their classrooms working with students. The ideal always is for school principals and assistant principals to be instructional leaders. In reality, the portion of time a principal or assistant principal spends in classrooms or in other direct, personal involvement with all teachers or with students who are not in trouble is usually minimal. What is to be done to bridge this partial divide? Please think of answers to that question as you read Case Study 4.1.

CASE STUDY 4.1

ASSISTANT PRINCIPAL: Our teacher evaluation system just seems to be so limited. We are required to observe half of the teachers one year based on the alphabet. Last names beginning A to K one year, last names beginning L to Z the next year. Two observations per teacher, right? So, with our block schedule a teacher has three classes each day. We have 180 school days per year. So, I observe a teacher for 2 classes out of 540 classes the teacher has all year. What's that show? That's less than 1 percent of the time the teacher teaches. There has to be a better way.

PRINCIPAL: I wish there was a better way. You are right—two observations per year is not much. But with three assistant principals, one principal, and 128 teachers, we have 64 teachers to observe each year. We will each work with sixteen teachers. We will observe our sixteen teachers. We will meet with them after each observation. We will have paper reports and a computer entry after each observation. While we are in the classroom observing, the phones still ring, the e-mails keep coming. The unscheduled person who has to meet with an administrator arrives in the office, something breaks in a science lab and we have to evacuate that room, a teacher gets sick and has to leave but no substitute teacher is available. The school board and the superintendent are seriously discussing increasing the observation requirement to four classroom visits per year. Two of the school board members have suggested that every teacher should be observed four times every year. Do that math—128 teachers, four administrators—32 teachers for each of us to observe. Four observations times thirty-two teachers means 128 observations per year. That means a class observation 128 times out of 180 school days. On more than two out of three school days you would have one observation, and you have a conference with each teacher after each observation. Plus everything else we have to do would still have to get done.

ASSISTANT PRINCIPAL: This is so frustrating. We know we should spend more time in classrooms, but who has the time. We're dealing with twenty-three hundred high school students, and the time demands on us are unlimited. When will the school board and the superintendent realize that we are asked to do more than is possible? Don't they realize what it is like to work in a school?

PRINCIPAL: That is so much like what teachers sometimes say about us. They wonder if principals and assistant principals remember how difficult it is to teach three classes daily for ninety-two minutes per class, keep up with grading all of the papers, keep up with all of the requests for data, attend all of the meetings and professional development, plan lessons, make all of the required accommodations for any student with any special needs, and make sure that every student succeeds plus that every student is 100 percent ready for the annual tests the state requires. So many teachers are convinced that school administrators just sit in our offices doing paperwork all day except when we attend meetings. The truth is, we don't spend enough time in classrooms, but with everything else we have to do that nobody else can do, what options do we have?

ASSISTANT PRINCIPAL: A friend of mine who is an assistant principal gave me an idea. He is at a middle school. They have seven classes each day. When he observes a teacher, he stays in one class from start to finish, and he stops by all of the other classes that teacher has the rest of the day. It takes some effort, but he says that he and the teacher can have a much better conference the next day because he has a better awareness of what the teacher does all day and, more importantly, of all the students the teacher works with throughout the day.

PRINCIPAL: You are welcome to try that. My dream has always been to make the rounds of the school each day during the first period. I would stop in each first-floor class on Mondays and Wednesdays. Then I would visit each second-floor classroom on Tuesday and Thursday. It rarely happens, but when it does, I really feel like I'm aware of what is going on at school. Well, it's time for us to go supervise in the cafeteria. That's our job and nobody else can do it. See you in the cafeteria.

THE PARTIAL DIVIDE

The partial divide exists within a school. Teachers spend almost all of their time at school during the school day in classrooms working directly with students. Sure, there is a pause for lunch, and there could be a daily planning period for teachers, but a teacher's day is primarily dedicated to direct work with students in a classroom.

Principals, assistant principals, school counselors, and other school support staff have different duties than teachers have. Some of those duties will include working with a student to resolve a discipline problem, to review progress toward passing a grade or graduating from high school, resolving some student-to-student conflict. Principals, assistant principals, school counselors, and other school support staff also have a lot of managerial responsibilities, duties and tasks that must be done for the school as an organization to function. Perhaps some of those duties could be assigned to a school business manager, to a school executive assistant, or to additional assistant principals. Sure, some people would complain about creating a top-heavy management structure, but when schools still staff their management structure and support staff structure identically to or very similarly to the staffing used twenty or thirty years ago, there will be problems. One of those problems is a continuation of and an expansion of the partial divide.

The school administrators in Case Study 4.1 discussed some of the day-to-day time management challenges they face. They also expressed concern that their superintendent and school board members may not have an accurate awareness of what it is really like to do the work of a school building administrator. What insights can teachers offer about their day-to-day work, especially what they would like to see? Let's listen to the voices of some teachers who responded to the survey for this book.

"If you could make one change in your day-to-day working conditions as a teacher, what would that change be?"

- "Less interruptions."
- "Less focus on test scores. More emphasis on learning for the love of learning."
- "Fewer interruptions. Too many instructional hours are lost in paperwork and testing."
- "Smaller classes, no doubt. Both teachers and students would benefit."

- "Have a one-hour planning period, not thirty-five to forty minutes."
- "No tolerance policy regarding extreme misbehaviors."
- "Make more effort to place chronic problem students in an alternative school. Those students need more help and attention than a regular school can provide. The students who do cooperate deserve to have the disruptive and potentially dangerous students in an alternative school."
- "More time. Longer classes. More time to plan, grade papers, and meet with other teachers."
- "Not so much emphasis on testing."
- "I would make classes smaller, extend the school day, and extend the school year."
- "Do away with the long holidays or reduce them."
- "Have more adults in the building, especially in the hallways. There could be volunteers, but they should be expected to enforce school rules."
- "Lower class sizes."
- "I would just like to feel respected and appreciated by someone other than fellow teachers, i.e., parents, administrators, the public."

What are the ideas that run through those comments? More pay? No. Better retirement plan? No. A major reform of the entire educational system? No. More technology resources and materials? No. Better school buildings? No. The day-to-day changes that were mentioned in those comments did not relate to more pay, more retirement plan benefits, a massive bureaucratic reform of the education system that changes everything in the workings of schools, more machines and gadgets and technology applications. Yes, more pay and retirement may not be daily thoughts, but they do relate to overall working conditions, yet there were no comments about those topics.

The emphasis was on providing more time to get the teaching job done. Another emphasis was on being able to work with smaller groups of students. More time to teach smaller groups of students means that in the day-to-day work of teachers the most important change mentioned in the above responses would impact what happens in classrooms.

There were also concerns about the emphasis on tests and on classroom interruptions. Again, these topics relate precisely to what teachers and students do in classrooms.

Chronically disruptive students are a clear concern. Teachers are concerned that these students consume so much time and effort while frequently disrupting class that there are two results: (1) the disruptive students do not improve or do not learn, and (2) the other students are denied the opportunity to learn at their utmost because of the classroom interferences that the incorrigible students create. Those disruptive students could learn elsewhere so creating more alternative schools could solve the tandem problems of how to educate the disruptive students and how to give the cooperative students the best possible opportunity to learn in the best possible classroom learning environment. These ideas will be explored further in the next case study, which adds details to a concern expressed in the Tuesday talk meeting in chapter 1.

CASE STUDY 4.2

Ms. CLEMMINS: It is time for us to get started. Thanks very much to everyone for attending today's curriculum and instruction committee meeting. Ten of the twelve teachers on our committee are able to attend today. I talked to the other two teachers, and they are involved with our school's academic team competition today. We invited our administrators to join us, and when bus duty is over, one of the assistant principals will join us. Well, there's Ms. Kelly right now. Thanks for hurrying from bus duty to our committee meeting. Now, let's start. We have two topics on the agenda. One, how can we minimize the many interruptions to classroom work, including students who are excused from class to attend some school-approved activity? Two, how can we return to an emphasis on learning instead of the current emphasis on testing? Let's take the first topic: interruptions. What are your concerns and your suggestions?

Ms. BROWN: The PA system is so disruptive. Why are so many announcements made during class time? We have to stop what we are doing, then listen to what was said, then get back to what we were doing. Then, later in the same class, there could be a knock on the door, and someone in the office has to see a student, so they send someone to get the student—can't that person come to the classroom and talk to the student in the hall so there is less class time missed. Am I asking too much to expect other people to do whatever they can so my students are in class?

MR. RONEY: The phone is what bothers me the most. As a teacher who floats from classroom to classroom, I have to answer the phone for every teacher whose room I use during the day when they get calls while I am using their classroom. Then we get other calls of someone asking me to get some message to a student. So classroom work is start, stop, start, stop as we go from teaching to the telephone to teaching to the knock on the door to teaching to the phone ringing.

MS. KARNISH: I agree with all of that. Plus, every day we get another e-mail about some vital school-approved activity that will allow a group of students to miss class. It might be that students are going to miss class that day and we got no advance notice. Of course, the e-mail always says that students are responsible for making up the missed work. How can the students make up the discussion we had in class? They can't. They had to be there for the discussion. Can't we put a limit on how many activities we allow students to be involved in that result in missing class?

MR. HUNTER: That's my concern, too. I plan my lessons very carefully. We work our way up to a test on Wednesday. I get some e-mail Wednesday morning about students who will be mentoring some elementary students today, and they will miss class. When do I give them the test? Do I have to create a second test so the students who miss class don't get test information from their friends to take the test?

MR. ROBINSON: I have some students who sign up to meet with almost every college representative who visits school. These students miss class after class, but sometimes they come to class, leave to go meet with the college representative, then return to class. That means class is interrupted twice. Can't we limit the number of college representative meetings a student can attend? How about having college representatives set up a booth in the cafeteria at lunch and meet with students then so classes are not missed or interrupted?

MR. LEBANON: Classes are interrupted too often for athletics or other extracurricular events. We have three or four athletic events going on each day it seems, and I'll get a call that a student must leave class early to go see the athletic trainer. Phone rings, I answer the phone, I tell the student, student leaves. We lose instruction time whenever this happens. I don't go to athletic practices or events and interrupt what they are doing by insisting that a student leave the athletic practice and come do a physics lab project!

MS. PHILLIPS: My concern is all of the students who roam the halls during class time. They knock on doors. They make noise. They create disruptions and interruptions.

MR. VON: Everything we are saying is true. All of these interruptions and disruptions get in the way of teaching. We keep trying new plans and programs to get test scores up, to get grades up, to get drop-out rates down. School is the program. We have no idea how effective our teaching could be because our school allows so many interruptions of classes and excuses so many absences from classes. Instead of next August being the start of another can't-miss teaching reform or innovation, let's just eliminate the interruptions and all of the excused absences. Having every student in class with zero interruptions could be the most effective educational reform ever tried. Plus, it costs no money, and we would not have to sit through any of the typically awful professional development training programs to be told how to do it.

MS. KELLY: I really do hear what you are saying. When the administrators approve the school trips, the mentoring programs, the assemblies, or other events that take students out of classes, the intent is not to interrupt or to disrupt your work. The activities that are approved always seem to serve a good purpose, but maybe they interfere too much sometimes with classroom instruction. We do reject some requests. Some people ask to make an announcement during a class and they are told no. Some people ask if they can have students attend some event or meeting during school and we say no. I guess it is hard to find the best balance.

MS. FINLEY: I'm not so sure that we are looking for balance. We are looking for the instructional time to be protected. Sure, there are some emergency interruptions or some unavoidable schedule conflicts, but it seems that defending class time has become our job when the burden should be on anyone who would do anything that takes away class time. Classes should not be interrupted when there are other options. No event should take students out of class when the event could be held before school, during lunch, or after school. Why should teachers have to defend class time?

Ms. GAYLE: Well, it is obvious that we have serious concerns about all of the interruptions that class after class after class keep throwing at us. Certainly the administrators and the office staff could establish some procedure to screen all requests to use the PA system during class time. People need to be told that their little announcement is not as important as 128 teachers and twenty-three hundred students doing their work without being interrupted.

Ms. CLEMMINS: We have heard good input from everyone. That's our usual approach. Our committee works well for many reasons, including getting ideas and perspective from everyone. One thought I would add. I have taught at this high school for fourteen years. I'm quite sure that in the past five or ten years we have more interruptions every year. That's the trend. More families ask for us to let their son or daughter leave during more school days for some appointment. For some reason, I notice more students missing several days of school for a family trip. I know that there are many more of the school-approved activities, field trips, musical performances, mentoring programs, and other projects our students are allowed to miss class for. Maybe the increased number one year to the next is not much, but ten years of this trend has created the current situation where we never go through a full school day without the phone, the public address system, a knock on the door, a school-approved activity, or a family request taking time from our instruction in our classes. OK, what solutions would you offer?

Mr. RONEY: Ms. Kelly, is there any procedure that the administrators, teachers, or office staff use to authorize use of the public address system during class time? I'm thinking that someone or any administrator should have to approve that. It seems to teachers that a lot of the times class is interrupted by some PA announcement, well, that it just was not necessary. We have morning announcements daily at the start of first hour. We sometimes have a quick PA announcement at the end of the day right before dismissal. Could we have some screening or approval process for any PA use at any other time of the day?

Ms. KELLY: I'll talk to the principal and the other assistant principals to consider that. I'm sure that it is very frustrating to have so many interruptions. There should be a way to reduce that, but I doubt that we can completely eliminate it.

Ms. Karnish: As far as all of the school-approved absences from class, we take attendance every class, and the attendance clerks put a label or description code on each absence. Could we put a limit of two school-approved activity absences per student for each semester? I mean a student could miss two classes in that category and no more. That way they have to select which activities are most important to them. As it is now, there are no limits so some students participate in just about every school-approved activity that includes any chance of missing class.

Ms. Phillips: My pet peeves are the phone and the knocks on the door. Can we encourage people to use e-mail during the school day instead of the phone whenever possible? I know that if a family comes to unexpectedly pick up a student, the attendance office has to call the classroom, but unless there is some immediate need like that, just use e-mail. We really have to insist on this for the benefit of teachers who float from room to room so they don't become phone secretaries for the teacher who is on planning period, but who is not in the room while the floating teacher uses the room.

Ms. Clemmins: These are good ideas. As always, I'll compile a summary of our discussion and of our recommendations for the minutes of our meeting. I'll e-mail those minutes to faculty and staff for their information and for their input. At our next meeting, we will review all input, reach agreement on our exact recommendations, and then make plans to present those recommendations to the school council for their consideration and action. Our next topic is how to return to an emphasis on learning instead of an emphasis on testing. What are your thoughts?

Ms. Brown: I'm sure that when the state government created our testing system they hoped it would measure learning, but that just is not how people look at it. The week of state testing is surreal—it's not school. There's school, and then there is that week. The students always comment on how strange the tests are. The students know a lot more than those tests can measure. We spend an entire week on those tests and almost nothing else gets done during that week. It's almost as if the biggest interruption in the school year is the week of testing.

Ms. Gayle: There is such an emphasis on the tests and the test scores. The state does not talk about learning. They talk about test scores.

When we finish that testing week in April, I always thought we would have some classroom activities in May that would be learning for the pure benefit of learning. That's difficult because so many students think that since the super-important tests are over, the real work of the school year is over.

MR. HUNTER: The test system is here to stay. We can discuss it, we can criticize it, we can offer ideas, but it is not going to go away. The state has spent millions of dollar on those tests, probably hundreds of millions of dollars. The state cannot say that the tests are a mistake.

MS. PHILLIPS: Some teachers from our school have been involved with the test review meetings each summer. I went to one of those meetings two years ago. Officials from the state department of education listened to our concerns about how many school days the testing takes, about the obsession with tests, about the test we use now being so different from the test of ten years ago even though the test scores of the past ten years are used to show our results over time. We told them how really strange a lot of the test questions are. The way the test questions are written is different from what most teachers use daily. It seems that the test questions are so, maybe, sterile is the word, or maybe they are just so generic, almost computer created instead of written by a human. So, after everyone provided input we heard four hours of education jargon speeches about the use of tests in states throughout the country and the wisdom of the testing system in our state. From what I can tell, that conference consumed time and money but produced absolutely nothing.

MR. RONEY: Let's be honest. The state government controls those tests. There is little or nothing that we can do.

MR. LEBANON: That's true. We would have to spend endless time communicating with the governor, the state legislators, the state department of education officials. Who has the time for that? If we had the time, there is still no guarantee of any change even after we make everyone in positions of power aware of the problems the test system is causing.

MS. FINLEY: Maybe we can't do anything about the tests, but we can do something to encourage an atmosphere where learning is treasured, is valued, is emphasized, is rewarded. The tests are here to stay. We have to improve each year on test scores. Why do we have to let all of that keep us and keep our students from being fascinated with learning?

Ms. Robinson: I wish that could happen, but the governor, the education commission, the superintendent, the principal always talk about test scores. The message they send is that nothing is more important than test scores. Do what works to get these scores up.

Ms. Karnish: I'd like to think that we can have both. I'd like to think that an emphasis on learning would result in improved test scores. As we have all been told, the purpose of a school is to cause learning. If we cause learning, the improved test scores should follow.

Mr. Von: Look at sports. The state does not test our students in their athletic abilities, but hundreds of our students work hard and get great results in sports, in band competitions, in chess team tournaments, in theater, in speech tournaments—those results always are rewarded. The newspaper has articles about high school sports. The morning announcements are sports, sports, sports. Coaches send e-mails telling us how well their teams have done. We do not reward students for their academic work as much or as publicly or as enthusiastically as we reward them for their touchdowns, their home runs, or their marching band competition successes. The state is sending the message that test scores matter more than anything else. Maybe we are sending the message that football game scores, soccer game scores, marching band competition scores matter more than anything else, including classroom learning. Think of every action we take to acknowledge, to celebrate what students accomplish. We put more attention on sports than we do on academics if we measure the effort, time, and emphasis we communicate through our rewards.

Ms. Kelly: To be realistic, the tests are here to stay. Still, we can promote learning, we can recognize learning, we can reward learning more than we do. We can be much more aware of what we communicate. We have to continuously improve test scores—that is just the political reality—but being obsessed with tests could be counterproductive.

Ms. Clemmins: Great discussion. Just like the interruption topic today, this topic is being discussed by our committee for the first time. That means we need input from all faculty and staff, so I will summarize our discussion on testing and learning in the minutes of our committee meeting. I'll e-mail the minutes to all of you and to the entire faculty and staff for their information and input. At our next committee meeting we will review all input and develop specific recommendations to present to the school council. Thanks very much to everyone for your time and work today.

The partial divide between teachers and everyone else who works at a school exists for many reasons. Teachers have a completely different job to do than the jobs that must be done by principals, assistant principals, school counselors, school law enforcement officers, school social workers, office staff, school maintenance staff, cafeteria workers, and anyone else who works full-time at a school. Teachers spend most of their time at school in classrooms working directly with students. No other person at a school spends most of his or her time at school in classrooms working directly with students.

Teachers know more about the classroom reality than anyone else who works in education knows. The classroom is where students spend most of their time at school.

The classroom is the only place where the highest priority of a school—to cause learning—can best occur day after day. The partial divide can and must be bridged so principals, assistant principals, school counselors, and everyone else working at a school are accurately aware of what can be done to better support teachers, what can be done to reduce or to remove obstacles that teachers face, and what impact every decision has on the classroom reality.

The partial divide exists partly because in the busy pace of every day at school, each person is attempting to do his or her job, which is often, if not always, too much to do in too little time. There is a very important efficiency in bridging the great partial divide. If administrators at a school make it a very high priority to not let classes be interrupted, then academic instruction can be more productive, more and better learning can be caused, test scores can improve. That could reduce the need for various remedial programs that the administrator would have to organize, manage, and evaluate. Your choice—eliminate interruptions or add a new remedial program? If that sounds too simple, try it before you make your final judgment.

Another reason that the partial divide exists is time. For the partial divide to be bridged, some time must be invested in more communication, more interaction, more consensus building among the teachers in a school and all other educators or staff members in a school. Again, there can be an efficiency. For example, I needed to make several seating changes in one class to resolve some misbehavior. I knew the seating changes would be responded to with defiance by a few students. I asked an assistant principal to visit my classroom on the day the seating changes were to be made. He came, spoke for two minutes to the class, watched as I implemented the seating changes. There was no defiance, and the behavior issues were resolved. The assistant principal saw the benefit of working with me for a few minutes in the classroom instead of having to work with the several discipline referrals I would have written about defiant students who resisted the seating change.

Did it bother me that I had to ask for help from the assistant principal? No. I know the classroom reality. I know the help I need. When I ask for help, the request is sincere and serious. The assistant principal knows that I realize the demands on his time. He and I bridged the partial divide. We worked together. We improved the classroom reality without any new law, tax, policy, or procedure. Sometimes education improvement happens simply because two people listened to each other and worked together.

CASE STUDY 4.3

The setting is in a middle school cafeteria on a Tuesday morning at 8:00 a.m. as administrators, teachers, and other school staff members are gathering for coffee and a light breakfast provided by the Parent-Teacher Association (PTA). Next Monday is the first day of school for students, so this will be a busy week. This is the first day that teachers were scheduled to be at school although many worked at school yesterday, donating their time. In fact, many teachers worked at school one or more days last week, again donating time. This case study begins with some of the informal conversations among teachers, administrators, counselors, and staff members.

ANNE MARION, ASSISTANT PRINCIPAL: Good morning, Taylor. People are early today. The start of a school year is always exciting. Are all of the new teachers here yet? I want to be sure they get introduced to as many other teachers as possible.

TAYLOR FERGUSON, PRINCIPAL: I think I've seen each of the new teachers. I talked to Robert Taylor, our new art teacher. He said that the new teachers got together yesterday to prepare a song and a skit for everyone, so we'll have that presentation early in the program this morning.

RACHEL HARVEY, TEACHER: Anne and Taylor, good morning. Or should I say Ms. Marion and Mr. Ferguson? I want to get everything right on my first day.

ANNE: Our teachers and staff are all on a first name basis, but when students are around, we always use "Ms. Harvey" or "Mr. Ferguson" to help students learn proper manners.

RACHAEL: That is exactly what I'll do. Well, I'm going to mingle. I've got the list with the name of every teacher, administrator, and staff member. The idea is to find out from each person what their top goal for this year is and to find out what their favorite hobby is. So I'll start with both of you. Anne.

ANNE: My goal is to see fewer discipline referrals. My favorite hobby is gardening.

TAYLOR: My goal is to see test scores go up. That's the only goal my boss ever asks me about. My hobby is—this might surprise you—mountain climbing. My family and I take a trip each summer to climb a mountain or at least to camp in some mountains. How about you, Rachael? We have the same sheet to complete.

RACHAEL: My goal is to have a great first year of teaching. I think what matters most to me is that there are no F grades and really no D grades by any of my students. Hobbies? Running. I was on my high school track team, and I was in a very competitive running club in college. Well, we all have other people to talk to, so I'll see you later. Have a great day and a great school year.

JAMES WELCH, COUNSELOR: Can you believe we have to play the fill in the sheet game? There are four families in the guidance office waiting to see me. Who has time for this?

CELESTE HAWKINS, SCHOOL LAW ENFORCEMENT OFFICER: I know what you mean. All of the officers in the district were told to attend every faculty meeting this year. It's supposed to help us be part of the school. I wasn't hired to be part of the faculty. I was hired to make the place safe for everyone.

JAMES: What choice do we have? Mr. Ferguson said in the e-mail that everyone would complete this sheet. So, what's your goal and what's your hobby?

CELESTE: My goal is zero crime. My hobby is coaching little league baseball. How about you?

JAMES: My goal is to never have as many as four families waiting to see me. It's embarrassing to have the office full. It looks like I'm not on top of my job. Hobby? I like to bowl. Now, I have to sneak back to the office. I'll get the rest of the information about people later. Goals and hobbies can wait. My work can't wait.

NED HARPER, TEACHER: Well, how are the sophisticated, artsy, superstar teachers today? Have you given your quartet a name yet? Let's see—band, orchestra, chorus, and art. Are you the BOCA group? Anyway, since the music and art people are huddled together, it takes an outgoing English teacher to get you guys involved with anyone else. Now, tell me your goals and your hobbies. Then go talk to other people even if they are not musicians or artists.

JULIE BROOKWOOD, TEACHER: That's easy. My goal is for more students to get involved with band classes. I need to fill all of my classes or my job will change and I'll get sent to another school. My hobby is obvious. Music. Music. Music.

BRIAN BARNHAM, TEACHER: The orchestra has been growing for a few years, but this year's sixth-grade numbers are low. Somehow I need to get a lot of sixth graders to be playing violins. That's my goal. Of course, music is my hobby, but my fiancée has gotten me interested in something I never tried before—French cooking. Maybe I can teach students to cook if I can't get enough of them to join orchestra classes.

DEBORAH LYON, TEACHER: The chorus classes I have at this school are packed. The classes at the elementary schools where I spend the mornings are set up for me. So there is no problem with numbers. My concern is that the school district might cut costs by reducing vocal music classes. So to be honest my goal is to prevent a cut like that. My hobby is to travel.

ROBERT TAYLOR: Well, I'm new at this school, and I'm new to teaching. I have hundreds of goals. To be honest, I just want to make it through the first day. I'm excited, but I'm nervous. I know I can do this, but it's still a little overwhelming. My hobby is carpentry. I make furniture.

NED: I'll make it easy for you. My goal is for every student to read, read, and read. It's that simple. No other skill in the English curriculum is as important as being a great reader. My hobby is—you guessed it—reading. Now, your classical quartet needs to move around and talk to other people. Go.

The goal and hobby project will create some conversations. Faculty, staff, and administrators will learn something about their colleagues. Some people may extend these conversations later in the day, week, or year. People with similar hobbies might start a faculty cooking club and provide fancy lunches occasionally. That could build some sense of friendship and team spirit. People with similar goals about reading could agree to trade the most effective reading instructional activities they create during the school year.

Other people will resent having to take time to complete the chart about goals and hobbies. Those people may see it as a contrived procedure to force people to talk and listen when they would rather work alone in their office or classroom. Not every person in a school is eager to listen to other people in the school. There are other activities that could be used to increase the conversational interaction among everyone during the first day back at school. A major point is that conversations, listening, and talking may need to be encouraged and organized.

Of course, the faculty, staff, and administrators would not stand or sit silently at 8:00 a.m. on that Tuesday in August if they are not required to interact about goals and hobbies. Friends will talk to friends. Colleagues who have worked together for years will visit with each other. New teachers will make alliances with other new teachers and some of the veterans will take the initiative to reach out to the newcomers. What harm is there in organizing an activity that results in everyone talking to everyone else? What are the possible benefits of doing this? How could this type of activity, done occasionally throughout a school year, help bridge the partial divide? What follow-up could be done to further bridge the partial divide? The next case study explores the possible benefits of personal follow-up.

CASE STUDY 4.4

Taylor Ferguson had been principal of Monroe Middle School for three years. He promised himself that the emphasis during his fourth year would be improved communication. It seemed strange to him that people at school complained that communication was inadequate because everyone was in the same building every day. How difficult could it be for people to talk, to listen, to communicate?

Still, the annual evaluations done by the school climate committee kept showing that faculty and staff members were dissatisfied with the communication at school. If that was the perception, whether Taylor thought it was valid or not, that was the perception. Some action was needed.

During the summer Taylor Ferguson talked to other principals, to retired principals, to central office officials in search of communication ideas. He read several books about how business executives improve communication with their employees. He searched online to find ideas about improved communication. His overall conclusion was that two areas of improvement could get the most significant results. First, Taylor had to make sure that he personally saw and spoke to each teacher every day. Second, Taylor had to ask teachers what their professional goal was for the year and ask teachers what they would like him to do to support their effort to reach that goal.

Taylor began visiting every classroom in the school often; in fact, he soon realized that he could make a very quick visit to each classroom during first period every day. The office secretaries knew that first period was Mr. Ferguson's time to make the rounds of all classes. This was not a formal observation. These quick visits alone did not equal total awareness or complete communication, but benefits could build as visits continued regularly. This was building awareness, connections, and insight. Once a week Taylor changed his visits to second-period class to see students in different settings and to be in classrooms of teachers who had first-period planning.

What amazed Taylor was not what he saw in the classrooms, although most of what he saw and heard was encouraging. What amazed Taylor was how many meaningful, productive, personal follow-up conversations he could have with teachers and students the rest of the day based on what he saw and heard while quickly visiting classrooms. When he supervised each day in the cafeteria, Taylor heard himself saying often, "Great answer in math class today, David," "Very impressive questions today in English class, Mr. Harper," or "Jason, are you sure you were really paying attention in first period today? I think you can do better. In fact, I've seen you do better."

The one hour of time invested in visiting every classroom, seeing every teacher, and seeing every student saved time for Mr. Ferguson. Getting Jason to pay attention helped prevent some disruption Jason might have caused that would have resulted in Mr. Ferguson having to deal with Jason's misbehavior. Discussions with teachers as they came through the cafeteria to get their lunch improved communication, meant problems could be discussed while they were still small problems, meant that many encouraging words could be offered, and avoided some meetings that would have taken more time if Mr. Ferguson and a teacher had to resolve a matter that had been allowed to fester.

Now, Taylor needed to work with each teacher on their professional goal for the year and what he could do to support the teacher's effort to reach the goal. At the September faculty meeting, Taylor reminded everyone of the August conversation activity. "We have been in school for one month. The goal you identified in August may still be your goal or perhaps during the past month of real experience with your current students, you have selected a different goal. That's up to you. You have a sheet of paper that is bright yellow. There are two questions on that sheet for you to answer now right after you put your name on the paper. Question one asks what your professional goal as a teacher is for this year. Question two asks you to tell me what I could do to support you in reaching that goal. Please think and write. Please be polite, but be straightforward. Most people smiled when they were reminded to be polite. Most people, also, were quite straightforward in what they wrote.

When the rest of the items on the faculty meeting agenda were completed, Taylor went to his office to read the yellow pages. "My goal is to manage time in class better." "My goal is to return tests and other papers to students faster." "My goal is to use a bigger variety of teaching methods." "In all honesty, my goal this year is to keep my blood pressure down. I love to teach, but the pace of this work keeps elevating my blood pressure." The comments were offered in a sincere, polite, and professional manner.

"I could really use some help with homework. So many of my students either refuse to do the homework or are late with it."

"My goal is for no student to make an F grade. How can I get that to happen?"

"My goal is to get grades entered on the computer faster. Can you show me some way to do that?"

"My goal is to get students to read more. I think it would be great if you read a book that my class reads and came to talk with them about it."

"Here's what I need for my goal. Turn off the PA system. Let me teach every class without any PA interruptions. My goal is to help my students learn how to pay attention, how to listen, how to be involved in class discussions. Nothing gets in the way of that more than those constant PA interruptions."

Taylor realized that what most people were asking him to do that would help them reach their goals involved time and ideas, not money. Taylor read the book that seventh-grade English students read, and he visited the class to discuss it with them. Taylor had the school's technology expert show a teacher some aspects of the grade entry software that simplify the process of entering grades in the computer. Taylor told the office staff that tomorrow would be an experimental day of no PA interruptions during class time. This led to a new schedule of PA announcements being made at the start of the day, right before lunch, and at the end of the day. This schedule virtually eliminated classroom time being interrupted by the unscheduled use of the public address system during any class.

At the end of the year, the annual evaluation arrived via e-mail for all faculty and staff to complete. Communication scores were up, a lot, but the benefit was not that communication was up. The benefit was that this was a much better school year by many measurements of grades, discipline, morale, and personnel turnover.

Taylor began to think that he should write an article for an education administration journal to tell other principals about the benefits of listening to teachers. He thought a good title for the article could be

"Listening—The Unheard of Way to Reform Education." He was pleased with his clever choice of words for the title. He was much more pleased with the very successful school year.

Teachers do not need to wait for opportunities to be heard. Teachers can take some initiative. Begin more conversations with colleagues. Share more ideas. Keep administrators informed of the realities in your classrooms. Invite the principal, assistant principal, and other school leaders to your classroom. Attend committee meetings. Send e-mails to trade great teaching ideas. Avoid faculty lounge gossip. Participate in the formal system of communication at your school. Talk to people, being diplomatic, polite, professional, and honest. As I always require of my students, "Be G-rated, legal, and ethical." Please remember that everything that comes into the brain should not come out of the mouth. Wisely edited statements are more productive than unedited statements. Unedited words may have to be eaten, so beware.

The ideas in this chapter address the partial divide at a school. The next chapter addresses the massive divide that is between schools and the rest of the education universe.

5

THE MASSIVE DIVIDE

Taylor Ferguson's experience with his effort to bridge the partial divide taught him, actually reminded him, of some essential truths of leadership and management. Taylor realized that some of those truths can get lost, buried, or overlooked as the pace of activity and the volume of work facing a middle school principal mean that every day is filled with reacting to problems. Taylor had intended to be a principal who pre-acted, meaning who provided the leadership and management that guided the school toward an intended, purposeful set of results, rather than providing only the emergency rescue operations that fill the day with constant responses to problems or worse.

At first, Mr. Ferguson doubted that he could fit an hour per day into his schedule for visiting classrooms. His conclusion instead became "How can I do this job without visiting every classroom often?" The efficiency amazed Taylor. This one hour each day of visiting classes seemed to prevent two hours each day of solving problems sent to him or of lengthy meetings. The short immediate interventions he completed while making the morning rounds minimized or prevented problems.

It is possible that everyone who works in a school is a direct report to the principal. There could be 40 faculty and staff at an elementary school, 60 faculty and staff at a middle school, 140 faculty and staff at a high school—all of whom report directly to the principal. Assistant principals can have areas of very important responsibility, but it is common that the bottom line responsibility for personnel matters at the school is fully given to the principal.

Do school district superintendents have 40 direct reports? Do state commissioners of education have 60 direct reports? Do governors have 140 direct reports? No, no, and no are the likely answers.

Mr. Ferguson found efficiency in personally and directly reporting each day to each person in the school who reported directly to him. He saw each teacher, every student every day. He expanded his morning visits to connect with all office staff, counselors, and support staff either during first period or during lunch. What initially appeared as more work to do became a way to accomplish much more in the same time.

The follow-up conversations Taylor had with students and teachers were cordial, productive, and symbiotic. It was very obvious that Mr. Ferguson and the teachers were talking more to each other this year. The same was true for Mr. Ferguson and students.

It was difficult to quantify, but there certainly seemed to be a growing sense in the school that the principal was much more aware of what teachers were doing in their classrooms, how hard teachers were working, how much more demanding the day-to-day duties of teaching had become during the ten years that Taylor had been an assistant principal and principal. Teachers felt more appreciated and more respected. Teachers felt that their ideas and their concerns were being taken more seriously. These favorable results were obtained within one school. When the goal becomes to have a similar impact beyond one finite school, can that goal be reached, and, if yes, what can be done to reach that broader goal?

The president of the United States, the Congress of the United States, governors of all states, legislators in all states, state level education workers, local school board members, school district superintendents, school district central office administrators or support staff, community leaders, interest group leaders, and societal reformers all have opinions about education, concerns about education, and various degrees of impact on education. What bases do these people use when they make decisions about schools or when they express opinions about educational issues? Are they listening to teachers, the people who are doing the work each day that matters most in the grand American crusade for better schools? Are they following a political agenda instead of an educational agenda?

Let's begin with some comments from teachers. The responses below are some of the verbatim replies to this survey question: "The executives of some restaurant companies work occasionally at restaurants that the company owns doing the jobs of cooking, serving, and cleaning. What benefit do you think could come if people who make decisions, policies, or laws about education would occasionally spend a day in school as a substitute teacher?"

- "I think it would give them more insight to what is involved in teaching—not just mastery of content and delivery, but the real challenges of meeting all the needs of children."
- "They would actually get to see what it is like. They would be able to understand what we mean by stress and time. They might also get to see that there are so many ways to assess kids without giving them tests!"
- "I think it would help them refocus on the individual student, which for so much talk doesn't happen at the highest levels. Too many policies are about protecting the institution, not about helping the kids."
- "I think it would open their eyes, especially about student behavior. I think they should be a guest teacher with lesson planning and grading for a week."
- "That is the only way they will see the behaviors of those students that they aren't typically exposed to; however, they still would not experience the demands of paperwork."
- "This should be a requirement. No matter how much experience they have, so many things have changed. New and fresh experiences in today's classrooms would give great insight into students' needs."
- "They would realize there are interruptions, changes in schedules, and that teaching content is sometimes not the most important thing, but listening to and getting to know the kids is most important. They'd also realize that there is lots of paperwork."

- "I believe they would appreciate more what we experience each day, especially if they had to serve in our various roles as stand-in parent, personal fashion consultant, and counselor, not just teacher, as we do daily. I also believe that legislators may realize that their expectations are too lofty. I would like for George Bush to teach for a week and then ask him if he still feels the same way about No Child Left Behind."
- "They would understand to some extent the demands placed on us and how much society's view of education has changed."
- "This would help immensely. Ideally, these policy makers would do this for a longer stretch. Anyone can hold students' attention for one day using a preplanned lesson. The real challenge is maintaining that focus."
- "I think that is a wonderful idea—maybe even a week."

What ideas, concerns, convictions, themes, and hopes emerge through those comments? Few questions on the survey had more intense replies. The sense of urgency is evident as if teachers read that question and thought, "Finally, the people who tell me what to do will actually experience the challenges of doing or trying to do what they have decided I should be able to do easily. Finally, the powers that be will begin to understand what I am dealing with daily. At last, these people will have to face today's classroom reality."

The comments from teachers express no resentment, anger, or vindictiveness. No comment dealt with "They would see that I should be paid more" or "They would realize that our building is overdue for renovation." The emphasis was that people who seek to impact the real work that is done in classrooms by teachers for and with students would gain new awareness of just what that real work involves. The hope is that the new awareness would lead to laws, policies, regulations that address reality. The hope also is that the new awareness would lead to fewer new laws, policies, regulations because decision makers would filter out more of the legislative, bureaucratic, and regulatory clutter that might make a good headline, that might create the illusion of important decisive action when the real impact was to impose another unproductive burden, which detracts from the real work that needs to be done in classrooms.

The next case study will be more creative, almost fanciful. It will seem to be far from the typical, the common, the likely. Please ask yourself this question while reading Case Study 5.1—if the idea of this case study is logical, reasonable, and beneficial, why does it seem so very unlikely that the events of this case study could happen. In other words, if the case study seems purely fictional, question why reality cannot become what the case study presents as much as you question the "that could never happen, that's so idealistic" nature of the case study content.

CASE STUDY 5.1

LIEUTENANT GOVERNOR ALEXANDER: Good morning. That was the 8:15 a.m. bell, so we need to begin class. Your U.S. history teacher left the lesson plan, so we'll begin that soon, but first I need to check attendance. By the way, I'm Mr. Alexander, and I am your substitute teacher today.

JASON: Mr. Teacher, I need to go the office. I'll be right back. OK?

Jason walked out of the classroom.

Lieutenant Governor Alexander was not accustomed to people abruptly leaving any meeting with him, so Jason's swift exit was a surprise. Mr. Alexander thought about pursuing Jason, but that would mean leaving the class unsupervised. He stayed in the classroom and finished taking attendance. While writing the names of students who were absent on the attendance form, two of the five students listed as absent walked into class. Mr. Alexander changed them from absent to tardy.

MR. ALEXANDER: OK, let's get started.

JESSICA: We're sorry. Our bus was late, and then breakfast in the cafeteria was slow.

MR. ALEXANDER: The instructions I have from your teacher explain that any student who is late to first hour must bring a note from the attendance office, so both of you need to go do that.

JESSICA: Come on, Marie. Let's go get our notes.

THOMAS: [As Jessica and Marie left, Thomas advised Mr. Alexander] They won't be back. They never stay in class when we have a substitute, and they are late almost every day. Same with that Jason. He sees a substitute teacher, and he's gone. The other Jason behaves.

MR. ALEXANDER: The topic today is the Declaration of Independence. We have a short video to watch. You have a worksheet to complete while you watch the video. Then we have a writing assignment. The last part of class will be a pretest on the Constitution of the United States. Your teacher says in the lesson plan notes that the worksheet and the writing assignment are for grades. The pretest is to show what you already know about the Constitution of the United States. Andrea, Mrs. Cooper's notes say that you are the video expert in this class, so would you please set up this video for us to watch? Thank you.

ANDREA: Sure. Do you know how long this video is? Mrs. Cooper always leaves a video for us when she is absent. I was just hoping that this video was pretty short because videos get so boring. OK, it's ready.

MR. ALEXANDER: This video is sixteen minutes long. Here's the worksheet for you to do while you watch. Everyone needs to pay . . .

PA SYSTEM: Please excuse this interruption. We need all students involved in the Jackson Elementary School mentoring project to come to the counseling office now. You will be leaving to go to Jackson Elementary School in seven minutes. Teachers, the list of those students was e-mailed to you this morning. If you have questions, please call the office. [Three students get up and begin walking toward the door. The other students laugh.]

MR. ALEXANDER: Wait a minute. Before anyone leaves for that mentoring trip, I need to see if your names are on the list. I'll have to call the office since I don't have the e-mail. [As it turned out, those three students were not on the list. They said they were just playing so they sat down.] Back to the video. Andrea, please start that for us.

Twice during the sixteen-minute video there were interruptions over the public address system. "Teachers, please pardon the interruption. The Jackson Elementary School Mentoring activity had to be rescheduled for tomorrow. Those students should be back in classes in two minutes." "Teachers, the fire alarm system is being worked on this morning. If you hear the alarm, please stay where you are unless we tell you differently."

The video was fairly interesting, at least it was to Mr. Alexander, who was a political science major in college, a very successful law school student, a respected lawyer, and an accomplished political leader in his community and then in his state. He had intentionally said nothing to the students about his job as lieutenant governor. He was at Lincoln Memorial High School today to be a substitute teacher, to see for himself what a day of teaching was like and to expand his understanding of issues in education.

While the video played, Mr. Alexander circulated throughout the room to see that students completed the worksheet. Three students paid no attention, went to sleep, and Mr. Alexander managed to wake them up without creating any major distraction. A few students scrambled at the end of the video to write in some answers on the worksheet. Mr. Alexander was not impressed with the worksheet. It was on a very low level of just filling in blanks with short answers that had been repeated by the video narrator and had been shown visually on the screen in large type. The only way to miss the answers was to intentionally miss the answers, which was exactly what some students had done. This thought went through Lieutenant Governor Alexander's mind, "What law can be passed to require all students to pay attention?"

MR. ALEXANDER: Thanks, Andrea, for rewinding that so it will be ready for the next class. Let's be sure you got the big ideas. First, hand in the worksheets you filled in during the video. Be sure your name is on your paper. Now, what is one of the big ideas from the Declaration of Independence? [The classroom was silent. No student volunteered to answer the question.] Jason, what do you think was a big idea from that video?

JASON: You know, it was about Thomas Jefferson and all that stuff. It was a long time ago.

MR. ALEXANDER: That gets us started. Now we have a writing assignment to do. I'll pass out the information you need. Notice, the topic is the Declaration of Independence, but you are going to relate that to modern times. The writing topic is "How does the idea that 'All men are created equal' impact the educational opportunities that all students have at Lincoln Memorial High School?" Let's be sure the question makes sense. Who has the question figured out?

RALEIGH: My guess is that since the Declaration of Independence said something about all men being equal, we are supposed to say if everyone at our school has the same, you know, chance at school.

KENT: I don't have any chance to make the basketball team. That's not equal. I can play basketball, but I'm not a superstar. I'm as good as most people on our team, but the coach would never pick me. He knows who he likes.

MR. ALEXANDER: That's a good start. We seem to have the topic figured out. Now, you've got ten minutes to write your answer.

Some students began immediately while other students just sat there. A few students talked about basketball, not about the Declaration of Independence, so Mr. Alexander told them to start writing. One student put his head down and was asleep in seconds. Mr. Alexander was not accustomed to people he worked with going to sleep during the workday. He woke up the student, who gave Mr. Alexander a look that said he would be asleep soon after Mr. Alexander turned his back.

At the end of ten minutes Mr. Alexander collected the papers. Just as he was about to distribute the pretest on the Constitution, a student's cell phone rang with a musical tone that the students really liked. What was Mr. Alexander supposed to do?

Leslie said, "I'm so sorry. It's off now. I'm really sorry."

Rather than call the office to find out what to do, Mr. Alexander decided he would get that information when class ended. He could not take the time now to deal with the cell phone if the class was going to finish the pretest.

MR. ALEXANDER: There are fifty questions on this pretest. Your teacher's notes to me make it clear that you are to do your own work silently with your eyes on your paper. Any questions?

JAMEL: Does this count for a grade?

ANDREW: He said it was a pretest, so it's not for a grade. Teachers do this so we stay busy.

MR. ALEXANDER: Your teacher is using this to introduce the topic of the Constitution of the United States and to identify what you already know about the Constitution. So, this is not for a grade according to the notes I was given.

TERESA: Well, since it's not for a grade, I really don't care. Here, you can have it back.

MR. ALEXANDER: Go ahead and read the questions. Most of them are multiple choice so you can figure out some answers from the list of possibilities. At least make an effort to answer each question.

For the next six minutes the classroom was fairly quiet. A few students finished the pretest very quickly. They had to wait for everyone else to finish before the class could do anything else. Mr. Alexander thought there had to be a better way to use this waiting time, so he wrote "Pages 97–104" on the board and told everyone to read those pages as soon as they finished the pretest. On those pages in the textbook, the students would find the U.S. Constitution in its entirety. Most students either did not have their book or claimed they did not have it with them. When the pretest was completed by every student, there were seventeen minutes left in class. The lesson plan said, "If you finish everything before the end of class, students may silently work on other classes, or you could lead a discussion about the U.S. Constitution."

MR. ALEXANDER: We've finished the pretest. I noticed a question about the preamble to the Constitution. We had to memorize the preamble in eighth grade. Does anyone else know it from memory?

Apparently not, based on the total silence. Mr. Alexander recited the preamble to the Constitution. Nobody said anything after he finished the recitation. Mr. Alexander began wondering what it took to impress these high school juniors.

The classroom door opened, and a state police officer, more formally called a state trooper, entered. The trooper walked to the back of the room and stood, almost at military attention. Every student sat up straight. One student nudged a dozing friend to wake up the sleeper. Apparently the students anticipated that one high school junior was about to be arrested.

STEWART: That was outstanding, sir. The preamble to the Constitution never sounded so good. You know, it's too bad that the whole school can't hear you.

Before speaking to Stewart, Lieutenant Governor Alexander had to smile. The presence of a state trooper had changed the atmosphere in the classroom. Trooper Covington was assigned often to travel with Lieutenant Governor Alexander. Today was no exception, so they arrived at school together and then went separate ways so Mr. Alexander would not create suspicions about his full-time job. He wanted the students to treat him as they would any other substitute teacher. Still, Trooper Covington had a job to do. The trooper was talking to ninth-grade civics classes today, but he continued to have responsibilities toward Robert Alexander.

Mr. Alexander: Thank you. I take the preamble seriously. I take the Constitution seriously. [The public address system never played favorites. The lieutenant governor and the preamble to the Constitution could be interrupted as easily as everyone else and as easily as all other subjects.]

PA System: One announcement before first-period class ends. Students, today at lunch is the last chance you have to buy a ticket to attend the student versus faculty basketball game. The game will be during our final class period today. You will report to class, show your ticket to your teacher, and then go to the gym when the announcement is made.

The bell rang, and students exited rapidly. No student slept during class change time. The least alert students in class were amazingly lively once the bell to end class sounded. Mr. Alexander had to move to another classroom because the teacher he was substituting for floats into a different classroom each class period due to overcrowding in the school. About three hundred more students attend the school than the building was intended to hold. The estimate for a renovation and extension project is $17 million. That will not happen anytime soon.

Mr. Alexander walks through hallways that resemble the sidewalks and intersections of New York City when a traffic light changes. Gridlock occurs at a few hallway intersections. More than the hallway traffic, it is the vulgar language that Mr. Alexander hears coming from all directions that is most troubling to him. Mr. Alexander sees one other adult and guesses that she also floats from classroom to classroom. He finally locates his next classroom and has about one minute to organize himself and his materials. The water break and the bathroom break he hoped would fit in after the first class and before the second class will have to wait. The bell rings and twenty-six high school juniors are in their seats or are approaching their desks. It is time to begin. Mr. Alexander turns to the attendance notes for this class. Everyone is here. He then turns to the lesson plan for this class. The topic is the Stamp Act. The teacher has left twenty-six sheets of paper, thirteen are stamped and thirteen are not stamped. The papers are distributed, and Mr. Alexander explains the price difference. The unstamped pages are marked "Price $1.00," and the stamped pages are marked "Price $2.00." The only difference is the stamp. Students will earn ten cents in their classroom currency for each correct answer they give. Mr. Alexander has a list of thirty-nine questions about the colonial era.

After explaining what will be done, one student proclaims, "That is not fair! I have to answer twenty questions to pay for my paper, but Tasha just has to answer ten questions to pay for hers."

Tasha: Shawn, I'll trade papers with you if answering twenty questions is so different.

Shawn: No deal. I can answer all of the questions. I just want to make it clear that this is not fair. You can make $2.90, and I can make only $1.90. It's not fair.

The thirty-nine questions were asked and answered. The students were then given a copy of the Stamp Act to read. Mr. Alexander read it while the students did and then led a discussion on the Stamp Act. The class then watched a ten-minute video about the Stamp Act. They had to take notes during the video, and the notes were handed in immediately after the video. The final part of class for twenty-two of the twenty-six students was to work in groups of two and write a colonial-era pamphlet for or against the Stamp Act. Taking the side of a colonist, a British merchant who feared colonists would stop buying British goods to protest the Stamp Act or the King of England.

The other four students left class to attend a meeting with an admissions officer of a nearby college. Mr. Alexander told them to turn in their pamphlet tomorrow. Yes, there was a PA announcement calling students to the college meeting and reminding students to show their permission form to their teacher.

With about four minutes left in class, the strangest noise was heard. Mr. Alexander looked at the students, and they answered his unspoken question. "Fire drill."

Somebody probably pulled the fire alarm. The building was quickly evacuated as Mr. Alexander followed his students because they know the routine. Trooper Covington caught up with Mr. Alexander to be sure that the lieutenant governor was in no danger. Students who saw Trooper Covington began to wonder if this was more than a false fire alarm. Everyone was told to go back into the building almost as soon as the evacuation was complete. As it turned out, a teacher saw the student who pulled the fire alarm as the teacher, unknown to the student, watched while coming around a corner. That student would be suspended from school for at least five days and perhaps ten days. Mr. Alexander began to wonder what other unexpected events would occur today.

While the students and teachers returned to classrooms, the bell rang to end second-block class. Mr. Alexander collected his materials and walked, more accurately bounced off people, to the next class. Third-block class included lunch so this class had thirty minutes of instruction, then twenty-five minutes for lunch. Then sixty minutes of instruction. Third block had four lunch periods squeezed into it. This was not the lunch schedule Mr. Alexander was used to. After the first part of class, he went to the cafeteria, stood in line, sat at a table with several teachers, and barely had time to eat. The bell rang to send this group back to class and another fourth of the students and faculty to lunch. The hallways were nonstop traffic during third block. The lesson plan for third-block class was identical to the lesson plan for second block. When third-block class ended, Mr. Alexander had planning period, but that changed at the last minute. A teacher came up and said, "Hi, I'm Mrs. Kenton. You're here for Mrs. Campbell, right. I hope she told you that she was going to teach my fourth-block class today. I have a doctor's appointment, and I have to leave. My class is in the room right across the hall. The lesson plan is on the desk. Thanks for your help."

Why not? Mr. Alexander was here to learn and teaching another class would be more revealing than anything else. The lesson plan stated, "This is a good class, but they have reading problems, so we use a lot of videos usually. Please use the two videos on the desk, and if you need more to do you can use the newspaper articles I copied. The articles are about possible changes in the laws about getting a driver's license. That topic really excites high school students."

The first video was made by the state government. The topic was highway safety. The opening statements in the video were presented by Lieutenant Governor Robert Alexander. The students looked at the video, looked at Mr. Alexander, looked back and forth again, and then realized that the man speaking in the video was their substitute teacher. They were really amazed. They listened, paid attention, and kept saying, "That's our substitute teacher."

Of course, the video had to be stopped once when the public address system filled the building with another announcement. "The student versus faculty basketball game will begin in ten minutes. You had to buy your ticket before now. No tickets are on sale at the door. Students who have a ticket may show the ticket to your teacher and then come to the gym." Four students were gone in a moment after Mr. Alexander checked the tickets. He thought that this was a strange way to raise money and wondered if having students miss class for a game should be allowed. He could work on that later. For now, back to the video.

The class discussion about the video was productive until one student commented about another student failing the driver's license road test. The name calling got loud, a push led to a shove, and the shove led to a fight, almost. Entering the classroom quickly from the adjacent room where he had heard the noise growing as push had led to shove, Trooper Covington arrived just as the shove finished. Those two students silently sat in the back of the room with Trooper Covington between them as they calmed down. Trooper Covington then escorted the two students to the office for further lessons in justice. Trooper Covington then checked with the lieutenant governor to be sure that everything was back to normal. He then returned to the adjacent classroom to finish his presentation about law enforcement. Mr. Alexander wondered what would have happened without Trooper Covington's help. Now he realized why the state teacher's organization was so adamant about school law enforcement officers in every high school.

Trooper Covington is not a school law enforcement officer or school resource officer. He was at Lincoln Memorial High School for two reasons: (1) to speak to several classes including, as it worked out, the class in the room next to where Lieutenant Governor Alexander was teaching during fourth-block class, and (2) to be available should Mr. Alexander need any help or security. The day of substitute teaching gave Mr. Alexander much to think about, including the haunting question "What would I have done, what could I have done to prevent or resolve a fight if Trooper Covington had not been there?"

In addition to Mr. Alexander's new awareness of the importance of the state teachers' organization priority that schools do much more in the areas of safety and security, including state support for school law enforcement officers, perhaps in a new partnership with local school districts plus local law enforcement and state law enforcement, what other issues in education at the school level and at the classroom level is Mr. Alexander now much more aware of?

I will begin the list and you will complete it, please:

1. For students to learn, they have to be in class. Tardies, meetings with college representatives, the student versus faculty basketball game all take students away from instruction in classrooms.
2. If schools are so crowded that some teachers have to float from classroom to classroom, the urgency of expanding school classroom space merits immediate attention. It is very difficult, if not impossible, for a teacher who moves from room to room to provide everything for students that can be done by a teacher who has one room to fully develop into an efficient and effective learning location. Plus, it is possibly a legal and equity issue because teachers who float from room to room have multiple time-consuming tasks that other teachers do not have.
3. What happened to manners? Why are so many students rude and vulgar? Do we need more character education? Are their families aware of how rude and vulgar some students are at school?
4. Does the pace ever slow down? Classes, lunch, classes, lessons, attendance, fire alarm, and more. When do teachers do the paperwork, the lesson planning, the computer work? What looks like an eight-hour-a-day job for nine months a year to the public is much more demanding than that. Do people in government, do typical citizens really understand what teachers do?

THE MASSIVE DIVIDE   97

5. Do teachers ever get to talk to each other? In every job Mr. Alexander has had there was ample time for colleagues to meet often and work together. When do teachers get to do that? How does a teacher know what other teachers are doing? Do teachers ever get to visit other classrooms and see different ways of teaching?
6.
7.
8.
9.
10.

Now, we can go one step further. Consider a day when Lieutenant Governor Robert Alexander is a substitute teacher at the school where you work. If you do not work at a school, then consider a day when Mr. Alexander is a substitute teacher at the school that you know the most about.

During his day as a substitute teacher at the school you are considering, what would make the most positive impression on Mr. Alexander based on what he does, what he hears, what he sees?

1.
2.
3.
4.
5.

Now think about the opposite. During his day as a substitute teacher at the school you are considering, what would create the most serious concern for Mr. Alexander based on what he does, what he hears, what he sees?

1.
2.
3.
4.
5.

Lieutenant Governor Alexander spends an entire school year substitute teaching one day per month from August through May at ten different schools, each in a different school district in the state. At the end of the school year he compiled some conclusions that he shared with the governor, the legislators, the state's commissioner of education, and with several educational organizations that Mr. Alexander spoke to during June and July at summer conferences, workshops, or conventions. The major conclusions Lieutenant Governor Alexander reached are as follows:

1. Being a public school teacher is more demanding, more difficult, more exhausting, and more complicated than I ever realized. Teachers have a tougher job than the lieutenant governor has.
2. There is a vast variety of activity in our classrooms. Some students and teachers are doing amazing work. Many teachers and students are doing good work or acceptable work. The problem is that a portion of teachers and students are not accomplishing much due to many reasons. There is no one solution for all of those unproductive classrooms because the reason for the problem in each classroom is different. A one-size solution does not fit or solve every size of school problem.
3. Some time in some schools is wasted. Other schools minimize or almost eliminate interruptions, activities that take students out of classes, or other excused absences. This is an area in which schools could trade ideas. No new law is needed. The schools that waste time need to figure out how to stop that or need to get ideas that worked at other schools and amend those ideas as needed.
4. Most students do what they are supposed to do most of the time. People who do not work at a school probably have very little awareness of the misbehaviors that some students are causing now. Teachers were heard in faculty lounge conversations dreaming of more alternative school options for incorrigible students. Those teachers make a very important point.
5. The paperwork is overwhelming. On some days of substitute teaching, I collected over one hundred papers from students. Grading those papers could easily take five, ten minutes each. Imagine five hundred or one thousand minutes of grading to do

day after day. It would be easy for a very conscientious teacher to work fifty hours weekly at school and twenty to twenty-five hours weekly at home. In the nine and a half months of a school year, a conscientious teacher puts in twelve months of work.

6. It is important to rethink the size of schools. High schools of over two thousand students can be very impersonal as can middle schools of over eight hundred students.
7. Before any additional state money is given to schools, it could be beneficial to require each school to evaluate how they use their time. For example, why should the school year be extended by a few days with all the financial costs that will bring if any schools are losing hours and days of teaching time for meaningless assemblies, pointless field trips, activities that could be held after school, or a variety of events that reduce instruction time right before a holiday break.
8. Based on informal conversations with teachers, there may be sufficient reason to question the benefit of what passes for professional development. I asked about fifty teachers to tell me what they think of the four days per year they are required to attend professional development programs. Almost all of those fifty teachers said that usually the professional development was a total waste of time. The topics they listened to presentations about rarely related directly to their daily work. The state and the school district spend a lot of money on professional development. We may need a very precise audit of that budget item and evaluation of that use of four days of time. One idea is to change two of those days to classroom instructional days.
9. My day of substitute teaching revealed more to me about the schools of our state than every report I have read from our state department of education, than every speech I have ever heard anyone give about education, than all of the statements I have heard made by hundreds of people providing testimony to legislative committees, and more than everything I have read in newspapers. It's almost as if schools are on one planet and everyone else talking about schools is on another planet. We need to find ways to make sure that everyone involved with education is talking about the same reality, not their perception of schools based on how education looks from their planet.

10. Some political leaders in the state are recommending a massive reform of education. We did that about fifteen years ago. I'm told that we also did that about forty years ago. I oppose a new massive reform of education because it will probably just be more of the same old bureaucratic restructuring. No two schools I substitute taught in are exactly alike. The state government cannot reform education with one huge new law that the bureaucracy implements, telling every principal and teacher in every school what to do and how to do it. Some democratic, decentralized approach giving each school freedom to create its solutions and responsibility to show results could be a better approach.

Please remember that before the reader began Case Study 5.1, we agreed that the case study would not be dismissed because it was unlikely to actually occur; rather, our questions would be, since there are benefits when public officials spend extended time in schools, why not expect that time to be spent in schools? The experiences that Lieutenant Governor Alexander had were revealing. The insights he gained and the conclusions he reached could be the basis of very productive discussions, recommendations, and actions. Are the demands on the time of any lieutenant governor so excessive that ten days per year cannot be allocated to one of the most important and most costly of state government duties—education? In the 260 workdays in a calendar year—52 weeks times 5 days—can a state official not spare 10 days, 4 percent of his or her time, to personally be involved in one of the state's highest priorities?

One very effective way to bridge the massive divide between classrooms and people beyond schools is for more people to spend sufficient time in schools to personally and to accurately know the classroom reality in particular and the school reality in general. The next case study further explores this idea.

CASE STUDY 5.2

SUPERINTENDENT TRUMAN: This has been a long but very productive school board meeting. I want to thank everyone for their patience, attention, and work. As always, our final item on the agenda is general questions or comments from school board members.

Ms. Elbray: I have one question. The company where I work recently completed a very helpful time audit. The idea was simple and was to find out how executives and middle managers in the company actually use their time during the day. Our company is in the restaurant business. We own seventy-eight restaurant locations, and we franchise almost five hundred more restaurant locations. There were some surprising conclusions and some expected conclusions. The biggest shock was that company executives and middle management employees in the home office spend very, very little time in the restaurants. Sure, we stop by one or two of the nearby restaurants occasionally, but that leaves hundreds of other restaurants in seventeen states total that we rarely see. That is changing. A major factor in the performance review of each executive and middle manager from now on will be how much time are they spending in the restaurants. Also, while in the restaurants we are required to do some of the tasks the restaurant workers do, talk to the workers about their job and about our company, talk to customers about the restaurant, and share lessons learned from each restaurant visit with other home office staff via e-mail.

My question is, for school district employees who work at the district office, how much time do you spend in the schools? Also, when you are in the schools, what are you doing? Do you talk to the teachers, do you visit classes, do you talk to students, do you speak with administrators and support staff? When you visit a school, do you share the lessons learned with anyone?

Superintendent Truman: My goal is to be in two schools each week. Our district has twenty-three schools in it, so my plan is to visit each school once per semester. Our assistant superintendent has some oversight duties for school buildings so she is at a school when a maintenance, renovation, or construction issue comes up. Some of our curriculum specialists, special education specialists, our federal programs manager, and our technology manager respond to requests from schools.

Ms. Elbray: That sounds a lot like what our company's executives and **managers used** to do, but we do a lot more now. We are in several **restaurants** every week. We travel to a different city every other

Wednesday to work in various restaurants throughout that market. There are about forty restaurants within a two-hour drive from here, so we visit some of those in the week we do not travel further away. We could go to the same restaurant every day and learn something new. So, what could be done to be sure that people who work at the district office providing services for schools actually spend more time in schools to know what services are needed and to know if what is being done now to support schools is really helpful?

ASSISTANT SUPERINTENDENT MADISON: Perhaps it would help for us to get a measurement of how much time district office workers spend at the district office, in schools, at the state capital, in the community, or other places. We could do an e-mail survey and have an initial report at the next school board meeting.

SUPERINTENDENT TRUMAN: That certainly could be done. Ms. Elbray, would that be acceptable?

MS. ELBRAY: Almost. My guess is that the survey will show that not much time is spent in meaningful, productive ways or at all in schools by most district office employees. Maybe some district office people have to be at the office all day, every day, but the office people who are certified educators need to spend a lot of time where education happens. At our company the goal is to spend more time where the workers fix the food and the customers eat the food. Your goal could be to spend more time where the teachers and students experience the education. So, in addition to the survey results, please include some recommendations for how you will increase time spent in schools by district office workers.

SUPERINTENDENT TRUMAN: We will do that. It will be a very interesting topic to explore further. Mr. Phipps, what else?

SCHOOL BOARD CHAIR PHIPPS: Any other questions or comments from school board members? No? It is late, but do speak up now if you have a question or comment. OK. Is there a motion to adjourn? Motion made by Ms. Elbray and seconded by Mr. Buckner. All in favor, raise your hand. Opposed, same sign. It's unanimous.

The next day Mr. Truman, school district superintendent, and Ms. Madison, school district assistant superintendent, met to discuss the e-mail survey and related issues.

MR. TRUMAN: What's the best way to survey everyone at district office to find out how much time they spend in schools? Do we survey everyone at district office or just people who are certified educators who used to work at a school before they moved to the office? Do we survey the secretaries and administrative assistants? Do we survey people like the school district attorney? She is a full-time employee of the school district, but she never was a teacher. What do you think?

MS. MADISON: I would suggest that we survey everyone at the district office so we can give the school board a full report. My guess is that we have to be prepared for some low numbers even from the career educators. With all of the meetings district office people attend and with all of the paperwork we do, the truth is that as a percentage of our total work time, we are in school buildings maybe only 25 percent or so of the time. That's a guess, but it is probably close to what the facts will show. It might be lower.

MR. TRUMAN: I would like to keep this survey simple so people can complete it quickly and easily with e-mail. The school board did not ask for a one-hundred-page report, so let's not make this more than the board requested. We need to ask if people are certified educators or not. We could ask if people are in a management position or in a clerical position. The question of how much time do you spend in schools could be done with a list of options that people select from such as none, one to five hours per week, six to ten hours per week. Let's ask how many hours per week people work so we can see the hours at schools as a percentage of total time? What else?

MS. MADISON: Let's ask for a statement about what district office people do at school when they visit a school. Let's also ask people to tell us how important they think it is for district office workers to spend time in schools. Also, we can ask people what keeps them from being in schools more often and what would need to change to make it possible for them to spend more time at school. We can include space for general comments on the topic.

MR. TRUMAN: Good ideas. Please work with our testing and research director to write the survey and then show the final form to me. This is Tuesday. Let's look at the final form early on Thursday. It would be great to e-mail this to everyone on Thursday by noon and have a deadline for responses by Monday. Set it up so the replies are anonymous, but so we know who has not replied. We can send an electronic reminder Monday morning to anyone who has not yet replied.

The survey results were quite revealing. The statistics provided some measurement, but the verbatim comments also spoke clearly. The classified employees spent from 0 percent to 10 percent of their time at schools. These secretaries, administrative assistants, entry level bookkeepers, and other very necessary office workers simply were rarely asked to go to a school and almost never requested the opportunity to visit a school. They do office work at the district's office. Their job descriptions said little or nothing about going to a school to complete any part of their duties. Management personnel, such as the school board lawyer or the district's technology manager, had replies similar to the certified staff members.

The certified educators from the district office included curriculum specialists, testing managers, elementary school and secondary school associate superintendents, some state or federal program managers, and other specialists. The most common answer was 20 percent to 25 percent as the amount of time spent in schools. No person listed any number greater than 50 percent. The second most common answer was 10 percent to 19 percent of time each week spent in schools. Ten percent means one-half day per week, 20 percent means one full day per week. Of course, 20 percent could mean some time in a school each day with 80 percent of the time each day at the district's office or some other nonschool location.

The verbatim comments were especially interesting to Mr. Truman and to Ms. Madison.

1. When you visit a school, how is your time at school spent?

"Talking to the principal, assistant principal, and maybe the office staff."
"Helping the principal solve some serious problem."
"Looking in a few classrooms. Talking to a few teachers."
"Attending a meeting to discuss a student's Individual Education Plan or some other instructional accommodations being made for a certain student."
"Usually inspecting some concern related to the school building."

"Analyzing test scores with the principal and with the faculty."

"Usually for a meeting, but while I am there I try to walk the halls, visit a few classrooms, and, if it is lunchtime, eat in the school cafeteria."

2. How important do you think it is for the district's office workers to spend time in schools?

"I have never been told that I am expected to spend time in schools. My job description relates completely to the central office organizational duties I am expected to complete."

"I know that some people in schools wonder what central office workers do all day. We do not have lessons to plan, papers to grade, or students to discipline. We do have tons of office work to do. If I spent any time at schools, I would never keep up with the paperwork and the deadlines at central office."

"It is important, but I am not required to do that. I concentrate on what I am evaluated on. I can keep in touch with people at schools with e-mail, phone calls, or just what everyone hears."

"I know people who work in the central office in other school districts. All of them have told me that if you are supposed to get into the schools, you are told to do that and you are evaluated accordingly. I have never been told to go to a school."

"It is very important. I could never coordinate the curriculum implementation throughout the school district if I just stayed in my office. My habit is to stop in one school each day either on my way to work or at lunch."

"It is beyond important. I've never understood why some central office workers insist on staying in their offices. Office work is easy. There is no central office job that is as difficult as being a teacher or being a principal. I always figured that my job was to help the school people do their job. That means I have to be where the school people are as much as possible."

"To be honest, who has the time? My in-box is full. My to-do list is too long."

3. What keeps you from being in schools more often and what would need to change to make it possible for you to be in schools more?

"My job description says nothing about going to schools. I do exactly what my job description says. Change my job description to include a requirement to visit schools and I'll be in a school tomorrow."

"It might sound like an excuse, but when I do go to schools, there is no place to park. Then the office staff is friendly, but sometimes they can't find the person I need to see. So, if we can improve parking and if we can help the office staff in schools find people, that would help."

"If I wanted to spend time in a school, I would still work in a school. School districts have central offices because some parts of what keeps everything going has to be done here. Call it bureaucratic, but that's the way it is."

"Time. I work about ten or eleven hours every day to keep up with all of the reports, data, and meetings. When would I get to visit a school? Who would take care of my reports, data analysis, and meetings while I am gone? Eliminate some of the weekly or monthly meetings when all we have to do is be told something, and then I would have time to visit schools. Some central office meetings could be eliminated, reduced, or done electronically."

"Maybe I pick the wrong times, but when I do go to schools and have an appointment set up, they are often late because of something unexpected they have to deal with. So if I have to sit there waiting, give me a laptop computer so I can get some of my other work done."

"I rarely go to schools because school people have schoolwork to do, and I have central office work to do. I think I'm in their way when I go to schools. If they need me to come out and do something, just tell me what to do, when, and where to do it. Otherwise I think a visit just adds to everyone's busy schedule."

4. Any other comments on the overall topic of central office workers spending more time in schools?

"The school board raised the question about how much time are central office people spending in schools. Are school board members going to lead by example and increase the amount of time they spend in schools?"

"What exactly would I be expected to do or be able to do at a school that would be helpful? The people who work at schools know what they need to do and they do it."

"I'd go several steps further. Why just visit schools? Why not take some of us out of central office and put us in schools? Why do all of us who work at central office have to come to this office building every day to do our office work? With all of the electronic communication options available, let's downsize central office, put us in schools, and get serious about providing services directly to schools."

"This is a bad idea period. Office work has to be done in an office. Schoolwork has to be done in a school. Office work is different from schoolwork."

"I'm not sure how to get this done, but I do know that the people in schools really resent it when they hear me mention that I get to go out to a restaurant for lunch. Teachers can't do that. Principals can't do that. Maybe I should have to go to a school cafeteria for lunch."

"Come on. This is just another public relations stunt. The school board must think the taxpayers will be impressed if they read a headline that says 'Bureaucrats Have to Go Back to School' or something like that. I really resent this. District office people work, but we don't get credit for the work we do."

At the next school board meeting, the superintendent was asked for an update on the question of the school district's central office workers and the time they spend at schools or the time they do not spend at schools. Mr. Truman and Ms. Madison provided a summary of the survey results. There was some discussion and then a recommendation that every central office worker who is a certified educator would spend at least one hour in a school at least three days per week. The superintendent would set the example and begin this immediately. This would be evaluated after three months to see how well it was working and to see how it could be improved. Some central office workers were already spending more than this much time in schools. Other central office workers would find this to be a major change in their weekly schedule.

After three months, what would you expect the results of this plan to be? What would the benefits be? What changes could be proposed after three months? What would teachers and principals think of this plan?

Superintendent Truman surveyed the central office staff at the end of three months. He asked the certified educators to evaluate the benefits of visiting schools, to identify any problems with this initiative, and to offer suggestions about how to improve the plan. He also surveyed central office workers who are not certified educators. He was interested to know if they had noticed any benefits from or problems with the school visit effort.

The certified educators were in three categories: first, people who always had spent time in schools so the new plan did not change their routine; second, people who rarely had visited schools, so the new plan did take them out of central office more and put them in schools more; third, people who never or almost never had spent any time away from central office to visit schools. The new plan was a dramatic change in their routine.

The evaluations were polarized. Most central office workers agreed that spending more time in schools made sense. Concerns included the requirement of three visits per week and the question of what to do at schools during a visit. Mr. Truman understood that some weeks might include four or five visits while other weeks might just have two visits. Some weeks have only four school days, so that was a factor. The schedule for visits could have some flexibility.

The what to do during a school visit question seemed to have an obvious answer to Mr. Truman. Observe in classrooms. Of course, stop by the office first, speak to the principal or otherwise let the administrators know you are there, and then get into classrooms. Whenever possible, talk to people. Have a topic in mind such as "How is the new computerized system for scheduling a substitute teacher working?" or "What resources would help you the most if you could have more teaching resources in your room? Books? Equipment?" Don't let that topic control the conversation, though. Listen to people. Listen to their ideas, concerns, success stories, and questions.

Another concern was expressed very bluntly. "OK, we are visiting schools more. So what? I still have my office work to do. This just adds hours to my work week."

Mr. Truman began to think that it could be helpful to use the school district's e-mail bulletin board system to share what was learned after each school visit. During the next three months the certified educators from central office would post a sentence to a paragraph summary of each school visit. The summaries would emphasize ideas, questions, problems, or success stories; however, the summaries would never include anything embarrassing or personal. If a visit revealed a personnel concern or other serious issue related to teachers, staff, or students, that information would be given to the principal before the visitor left the school.

The input from central office workers who are not certified educators was fascinating. "When can I start visiting schools?" "The people I work with have different conversations now. They talk about specific schools and not just about schools in general." "I think these visits help remind central office workers what we are all supposed to care about." "Finally, people seem to remember that schools are the priority. Central office exists for the schools. The schools do not exist for central office."

When Mr. Truman and Ms. Madison reviewed all of the input, two conclusions stood out. These conclusions would be what they emphasized in their report to the school board.

First, less time can be spent in central office talking about teachers if more time is spent in schools talking with teachers.

Second, less time can be spent in central office meetings trying to figure out ways to improve schools if more time is spent in schools seeing what is being done, what works, what is not working, what the actual school conditions are today.

For Superintendent Truman this three-month process had reminded him of what he had long known about education, about leadership, and about management. Long before there were central offices, state departments of education, and the U.S. Department of Education, students were learning in schools where teachers taught effectively and directly. The bottom line in education is what teachers and students do in classrooms. Education happens in classrooms, not in bureaucracies.

School administrators and school district administrators—principals, assistant principals, superintendents, assistant superintendents, various directors, managers, or specialists—have demanding jobs to do. Some books or articles about the job of a school district superintendent use the word "politics" as much as or more than the words "education," "school," "teacher," or "student." The political process and public education certainly do interact continuously, but education is for learning, not for politics.

Motives matter. Motives vary. Motives lead to actions. Beware community groups, interest groups, political parties that seek to impact education. A political candidate seeking his or her political party's nomination for governor may promise a 10 percent salary increase for teachers but may offer no funding process other than to save money making government more efficient. What is the motive of a person who makes a political promise that cannot be kept? Beware.

Another candidate for a political party's nomination for governor promises the most comprehensive, top to bottom overhaul, reform, and restructuring of education the state has ever seen. It is possible, perhaps likely, that this candidate knows little about the history of massive bureaucratic education systemic overhaul, reform, and restructuring. In the midst of political groups, interest groups, community groups, and the media obsession with how the reform will redistribute power and authority over education policy making or law implementation, the day-to-day work in classrooms is given minimal attention by those same political, community, interest, and media groups. Beware.

What is the motive of a vocal crowd that packs the room during a school board meeting, which makes sure its representatives speak to all reporters, but which has no members who have been in a school recently? What basis does that crowd have for its collective opinion about schools if no person from the crowd has accurately identified the current reality in schools? Beware.

Making headlines about education is easy to do. Making a meaningful difference in the quality of work done in a school is much more demanding and is much more important. The headline makers from political parties, interest groups, or community groups far too often are severely separated from the classroom reality. "Our schools must become the best in the world" could be a generic statement by a political or community leader. Can that person then identify exactly what action needs to be taken in which classroom to get the desired result? No, so beware.

Political leaders, interest groups' leaders, community activists, journalists who agree that "Our schools must become the best in the world" typically spend very little time in those schools they make headlines about or write headlines about. They could visit schools. They could talk to teachers. They could substitute teach. They could help bridge the massive divide.

CASE STUDY 5.3

BEST. Better Education Starts Today. The community leaders were convinced that improving schools was an urgent, cannot wait, tomorrow-is-too-late priority. These same community leaders were convinced also that efforts to improve schools could not be temporary; rather, every day had to be yet another today when schools did their best work, even better than what only yesterday had been the best yet.

The communication had been sent through the old-fashioned mail service, through e-mail, through radio and television public service announcements, through media responses to several press releases that resulted in press coverage before the summit meeting, during the summit meeting, and after the summit meeting.

The first press release was short and blunt: "The community leaders and the citizens of Newtown will gather for a summit meeting on education. The highest point on a mountain is the summit. The highest level of attention in our community must be given to education. The organizing group of this summit meeting is called BEST, which stands for Better Education Starts Today. Please attend the summit meeting on August 1 at 7:00 p.m. at the gymnasium in the Franklin Village Community Center."

The summit meeting began at 7:00 p.m. precisely. The community center was packed. Parents, guardians, students, leaders of community organizations, members of neighborhood groups, elected public officials, candidates for public office, citizens, some teachers and some school administrators, many news reporters were there.

Audience members had been given the opportunity to sign up if they would like to speak to the audience. Fifteen people put their names on that list. The official program included three community leaders who would speak after the audience members spoke. When the speaking concluded, the self-appointed president of BEST would explain the action plan for everyone who would like to remain involved. The names of the audience members who asked to speak to the gathering were read and those fifteen people walked to the front of the gymnasium to line up. One minute per person was the time allotted for this portion of the summit. A sampling of the fifteen comments is below:

"Something is wrong in the schools. I have a son in high school and a daughter in middle school. They never bring any homework to do at home. They say they don't have any homework. Then they get an F or a D grade in classes on their report card. Isn't somebody at the school checking to see if students do their homework?"

"I represent the United Citizens Council of Newtown. We're a new group that speaks up for people who are never heard. Our members are concerned that some students in our schools are making perfect grades, getting the big scholarships, and doing great while too many other students are overlooked, are failing, are in the way, I guess, so people try to pretend they aren't there. We demand justice for all students. We demand equal protection of the laws. We think the rich are getting richer, the smart are getting smarter, and the children of the families who live in the right zip codes are getting more than they deserve."

"My concern is the school buildings. The new buildings are impressive, the old buildings are barely tolerable. How can students and teachers do their best work if they are in some of the worst buildings in town? Can't we do something so when a new school is built with everything that is state of the art, we simultaneously update the other schools to the same standard so it does not matter so much where you live? Otherwise only the few students at the newest schools will have the best resources."

"I've been to meetings like this for decades. Nothing ever changes. The schools that get good results keep getting good results. The schools that are weak remain weak. Some students succeed, others get by, still others drop out. Some families get involved and take the responsibility to make sure that their children read, do homework, study, watch very little television, have meaningful experiences in the summer, and get enough sleep. Other families blame the schools or the system or the national government. Making our schools the best they can be really means each family being responsible for their children and not expecting schools to do absolutely everything."

"Enough is enough. When I take my car to the local car dealer where I bought it and I need some repair work done, I don't sit there and watch the mechanic do the work. It is their job to fix the car and that's what they do, or I get so loud and difficult that they can't fix it fast enough. When I send my children to school, I don't go with them to be sure the schoolwork gets done. That's for the teachers and the principals to do, but is it getting done? I don't think so. Somebody tell me why those people who work at the school call me when my son or daughter acts up at school? I don't call the teacher when my children act up at my house. Enough is enough. Teachers are unfair to my children. Everybody knows that the schools are unfair. Some students get taught, and other students get ignored. Enough is enough."

"I do a lot of volunteer work in two schools. I see a lot, and I hear a lot. You have to be there to really know what is going on. I see every time I am at a school that some students work, cooperate, and learn. Some other students are disruptive and never work. Every student who comes in every school is given the opportunity to work, to learn, to study, to think, to succeed. Perhaps each family needs to have its own family summit meeting."

There were three speakers whose names appeared on the official program for the summit meeting. These speakers agreed to keep their comments to a very few minutes each. Their speeches follow.

"Good evening. Thank you for being here. My name is Marie Lynn Knight, and I am an assistant professor of education policy, supervision, and curriculum at Birmington Regional Community College. I am also a founding member of BEST. I should add that on Fridays from 4:00 p.m. until 8:00 p.m. I supervise the Unlimited Potential Scholars Academy at Birmington United Community Church. That program is designed to challenge students who seek a serious academic program at their school but usually find that school is easy so they get bored and make bad grades.

"In my duties as a professor, I am expected to stay fully informed about efforts throughout the nation that are seeking to improve schools. State governments, local school boards, corporations, governors, some mayors, some city councils, state school boards throughout this nation are trying various systemic changes in a search for ways to improve schools. Some recent reforms I have researched include same-gender classes in middle schools, separate ninth-grade centers for high school freshmen, grouping grades kindergarten through middle school together in one building, alternative calendars to reduce the length of summer vacation time away from school by using a quarter or trimester plan, and many others.

"The most impressive studies I have read show that any of these reforms can work or can fail. What matters most seems to be a combination of what reform is used and how that reform is implemented. Great implementation of a bad reform will not make the reform work but does make evaluation of the reform more precise.

"I leave you with this thought. If we were starting education all over again, what we would create for a new school system would have much that is different from what we have now. We can regret the inertia that has resulted or we can bravely make the changes to go from the education system we have now to the better system we would have if we were not locked into the status quo."

"My name is John Jennings. I was a middle school teacher twenty-three years ago for three years. For the past twenty years I have used my knowledge of math and of computers to become the chief information officer of a large regional bank company. I left teaching for two reasons. One, no matter how hard I worked or how many extra hours I worked or how many extra supplemental duty jobs I did for more pay, some other people in my school who worked fewer hours and just coasted in their classroom made much more money than I did. To properly take care of my family I could not wait ten to fifteen years to finally get my income up. I went into business, and it has been a good career, plus I have been able to take better care of my family financially.

"Two, the stronger reason that I left teaching was the bureaucracy. The state government kept telling us what to do. The school board kept telling us what to do. If you had an idea for your school or your school district, it could take forever to get anything changed. The bank corporation I work for moves at the speed of the business marketplace. Business has to change constantly to keep up, to take the lead. Schools seem to be about a generation behind in so much of what they do.

"Better education starts today by getting schools up to the technology standards of today, up to the building standards of today and up to the personnel pay standards and methods of today."

"My name is Theodore Jefferson Hamilton. I have attended far too many of these meetings in my seventy-seven years of living. All of the meetings are the same. People gather with lots of energy and excitement. People present opinions, concerns, accusations, criticisms, some accurate information, and a lot of inaccurate information. It is good for all of us to gather in a community center, listen to each other, look for solutions to problems, and then see what can be accomplished, but usually very little happens.

"Most of these meetings are much more talk than action. I'll prove that. Except for those of you who work in a school, please raise your hand if you have spent one full day in a school during the past year. It looks as if there are seven of you who raised a hand. That means about six hundred people did not raise a hand. Maybe 100 of you work in schools, so 493 out of 500 people here have not spent a day during the past year in a school. I'm old enough to have earned the privilege of being very straightforward. People who do not spend time in schools may make the loudest noises about schools, but those noises are far removed from the facts.

"If better education starts today it needs to start with all of you spending enough time in schools to be able to talk wisely and accurately about schools."

"My name is Allen Christopher. I'm the executive director of BEST. My job tonight is to help us decide what our next steps should be. To assist with that, I've asked two members of the BEST board of directors to listen closely to everything said tonight and to offer their perspective on what we should do next. Ms. Stephens and Mr. Thompson, what have you concluded?"

"I'm Belinda Stephens. My recommendation is that we take the sign-in sheets showing everyone who was here and send a follow-up summary of tonight's presentation to everyone. We would also send a survey to ask for input from everyone. Maybe we will ask for your ideas about the three most important problems in our schools and what you suggest we do to solve each problem." People politely applauded.

Mr. Christopher stood up. "Why wait? Let's do that now. Let's give everyone a sheet of paper. Put your name, address, phone number, and e-mail address on it. Then give your ideas on three problems and solutions. Since better education starts today, let's do the survey right here today."

"I'm David Thompson. My recommendation is that everyone here tonight who does not work in a school find the time to spend half of a day, at least, although a full day is better, in a school during the next month. BEST is scheduled to meet again one month from tonight, so do not wait until the day before we meet to go visit a school. At our next meeting we can divide into groups based on whether you visited a high school, middle school, elementary school, technical/vocational school, or alternative school. Be sure to call the school, schedule your visit, and get into classrooms. Don't just show up. Educators are professionals. You schedule a meeting with a lawyer or an appointment with a physician, so show educators the same courtesy."

What was likely to happen when BEST held its next community meeting one month later? Would current and future political candidates attend in search of votes? Would community activists attend in hopes of being part of the news media coverage of the event to solidify their position as a community activist? Would teachers attend or would they be at home grading papers and preparing lessons? What would the survey results show about the three most important problems facing schools and the proposed solutions? What had visitors to schools noticed as they spent a day observing in the schools throughout the community? Would the next meeting be a time when people reason together, seek shared concerns, and make mutual commitments? Would the next meeting be more accusations than ideas, more complaints than suggestions, more blaming other people than accepting personal responsibility, more performing for the television news cameras than sincere search for truth?

As it turned out, the most important decision made at the next BEST meeting was to change the name of the group. A teacher at the meeting was very persuasive with her appeal. "I'm a teacher. I've been a teacher for fifteen years. I'll be a teacher for at least fifteen more years. To be honest, I know more about teaching than you do. I realize you have concerns. I realize you are aware of problems. For many of you there is a genuine motive to improve schools. For some of you the motive is your ego, your career, a political campaign, or some score to settle with the school district. Well, here's my idea. BEST needs to stand for Better Education Success Together. Schools do not improve because of community confrontation. Schools have a better chance to improve through comprehensive community cooperation. Let's team up to create better education success together."

Cheers greeted that request, and the name change was approved. To show that this was not a superficial name change only, the BEST meeting organized a buddy system. Each school in the school district would team up with three buddies—a business, a community group, and a media outlet (television station, radio station, newspaper, neighborhood newspaper, cable television company, website, blog). The three buddies would visit the school once per week to provide help as needed for publicity, fund-raising, guest speakers, resources. It is amazing how much furniture, technology equipment, and office supplies local businesses continually replace that could be given to schools! The buddies were now in schools regularly enough to see the real needs and to easily arrange for donations. All of this was done with no new taxes, no new laws, no new policies, no new bureaucracy. All of this was done with the intention of having a direct impact on schools, especially on classrooms, because that is where better education success happens.

Some massive divides in our society have been reduced or have been removed. The Internet has created an e-bridge that instantly propels information from source to user. Cell phones enable instant communication from almost any point A to almost any point B. The global economy often transcends boundary lines between nations and political variations among nations.

There remains a massive divide between the classroom reality in our schools and the accurate understanding of that classroom reality by many political leaders, journalists, state education bureaucrats, school board members, local school district central office workers, community leaders, community activists, interest group leaders, and parents/guardians. These people do not work in classrooms, so they are not amid the classroom reality; however, when these people seek to impact schools they serve themselves best by identifying what the school reality is in general and what the classroom reality is in particular.

For any effort to improve education to work, that effort will have to be implemented in classrooms. Some reforms of education that merely rearrange the bureaucratic system may make headlines but do not make any improvement in learning. Those reforms waste time, effort, and money. Some reforms that merely import an idea from another nation, state, school district, or school can fail because what the idea did was not what the school the idea was being imposed on needed. The medicine that makes you healthy could make someone else ill.

The great divide can be bridged. For real improvement to occur in education, the great divide must be bridged; otherwise efforts will be random, disjointed, awkward, frustrating, temporary.

Step 1 in bridging the great divide is to listen to teachers.

Step 2 in bridging the great divide is to listen more to teachers.

Step 3 in bridging the great divide is to keep listening to teachers. Notice, this step is continuous.

Step 4 and beyond will include democratically making decisions, effectively implementing those decisions, evaluating the results of the implementation, and then, with a lot of listening first, making adjustments.

The classroom reality is what only teachers know about education. The classroom reality is the starting point for real improvement in education. Classrooms are not secluded, hidden, or isolated. Teachers are very willing to talk. Listen to teachers to learn what only teachers know about education. Visit classrooms to see for yourself.

Listening to teachers does not mean giving every teacher everything he or she requests. Listening to teachers does not mean making changes because of every complaint expressed by any teacher.

Listening to teachers does mean that before any change is considered or made in education, vast teacher input is obtained. It is honorable to include teachers in shaping their profession, their schools, their classrooms. It is efficient to include an accurate understanding of the classroom reality as a foundation for serious consideration of any effort to improve schools. Of course, input from people other than teachers is important as ideas are sought and as consensus is built. That is how democracy works and our public schools are part of the democratic system and process.

Listen to teachers means exactly that—listen to teachers. Listen sincerely, listen continuously, listen seriously. Listening to teachers is one essential part of bridging the massive divide.

In our next chapter the classroom reality will be explored, visited, encountered, embraced, evaluated, prepared for, and described.

6

TODAY'S REALITY

Have You Been in a Classroom Recently?

"The interim associate assistant director with responsibility for the Future Education Achievement Results (FEAR) task force subcommittee on the twenty-first-century curriculum, instruction, and assessment announced that the department of education's Office of Regulation, Compliance, and Enforcement would promulgate and disseminate regulations and procedures that school districts would create implementation policies for to be effective ninety days after the promulgation and dissemination."

The above fictitious statement sounds far too possible. The above statement is what education bureaucracies probably proclaim occasionally. Such statements are a foreign language and abstract concept when contrasted with the reality of what is done in classrooms or with the reality of how to improve what is done in classrooms.

"Those promulgated and disseminated regulations changed my teaching career into the dream job I had hoped for and improved student achievement beyond anything I have ever seen." That statement is also fictional. Why? Because student achievement is not determined by promulgation and dissemination of regulations. Student achievement is enhanced when teachers cause more and better learning to be experienced by students.

Bureaucracies promulgate and disseminate regulations. Bureaucracies create task forces with multiple subcommittees that publish reports, studies, and executive summaries. Subcommittees have meetings that spawn more subcommittees. Task forces have meetings that spawn more task forces. All of this bureaucratic busyness occurs miles away from schools where the real work, the essential work of education is done.

Bureaucracies are necessary given the size and sophistication, the complexity, and the multiple jurisdictions of the education universe in particular and of society in general. Perhaps the one-room schoolhouse was the only educational organization that could function with little or no bureaucracy. One challenge in the complicated maze of the education bureaucracy is for the bureaucratic structure to support education rather than support the bureaucracy only or primarily. It is too harsh to say, "Eliminate the education bureaucracy, and schools will still function." It is not too harsh to say, "The bureaucracy exists to serve the schools, the educators, and the students. The schools, the educators, and the students do not exist to serve the bureaucracies of the school district, state department of education, or national government department of education."

Have you been in a classroom lately? Governor Thomas, have you been in a classroom lately? State Commissioner for Education Simpson, have you been in a classroom recently? State and local school board members, have you been in a classroom lately? Education officials from the state department of education or the national department of education, have you been in a classroom lately? School district leaders who work in the district's central office, have you been in a classroom lately; in fact, since you are so close to schools, your question is have you been in a classroom today?

"Well, sure, we had a walk-through and a photo opportunity when the high school renovation project was completed in Brunswick County. We looked at several classrooms and spoke with teachers and students during the thirty minutes we were there. That was four months ago, so that fits in the lately category."

"Sure, I get into a school once a month. My office in the state department of education is a busy, busy place, but I visit one school every month for at least an hour. I talk with the principal, look around, and walk through a classroom or two."

"Yes, our school district superintendent requires us to visit schools often. She sets the example. We have fifteen schools in our district and our superintendent is in each school once every five weeks. She visits three schools per week during the school day and then gets to some of the after-school events or performances."

"No, I have not been in a school lately. Getting away from the office is almost impossible. I do read one or two school websites each day, and that is always very informative."

Have you been in a classroom recently? The only way to truly understand the classroom reality is to spend time in classrooms and then talk to teachers about what is occurring in classrooms. Virtual visits are inadequate. Rare visits are insufficient. Reading the executive summary of the most recent test data is superficial.

People who seek to improve education must know the classroom reality. Teachers know the classroom reality better than anyone else. What would current teachers like for future teachers to know about the classroom reality that their teacher-preparation program in college may not give sufficient attention to? The research for this book offers insights that those future teachers need to know; however, other people who seek to impact education can also benefit from these insights that come straight from teachers who live each day in the current classroom reality. The survey question and the answers that follow provide essential realities.

"What reality about teaching do college students who are preparing for a teaching career need to know that, perhaps, they are not being told sufficiently?"

- "New teachers are not taught behavioral classroom management. Teachers have to deal with many students who have emotional, social, and learning challenges."
- "Educational theory is not as important as actual, practical application of teaching methods. A wide variety of teaching materials and styles is needed."
- "Most of your students don't want to be there. No matter how cool you think you are, your students will prefer that you set limits for them."
- "You must have patience and realistic expectations and then more patience. Also, expect that some students will truly despise school,

and then you must get creative as to how you find ways to make it tolerable for them."
- "The paperwork is more than I ever imagined. Teachers have to be flexible because nothing ever goes as planned."
- "Teaching today is nothing like the ideals you have in your head. I had preconceived notions based on what I remember as a student."
- "College does not give you enough classroom management experience. Your first year teaching will take all of your time. The next years will be better, but it is not an 8:00 a.m.–4:00 p.m. job. You could work at school every night until 7:00 p.m. and still not complete everything."
- "Management. They need more instruction with it and with lesson preparation. Methods classes did not prepare me for reality."
- "That teaching is a 24/7, 365-days-a-year job."
- "If you do not have behavior management skills you are going to have a very hard time."
- "That being a teacher means that giving 110 percent is not enough—someone always wants more."

What topics were emphasized in those survey responses? Management of the classroom is increasingly demanding and difficult because more students today bring with them everything from a hatred of school to a real or claimed condition, syndrome, limitation that requires significant effort, attention, and intervention to be implemented simultaneously, yet inconspicuously.

The responses also emphasized the large amount of time that is needed to teach well in today's classroom, to prepare lessons, to grade papers, to complete all paperwork.

For people who have been to a classroom lately and who regularly visit classrooms for thorough observations, the classroom management reality and the time reality may be clearly understood.

For people who rarely or never visit a classroom, the reply to these areas of concern could be, "It's just a group of students. How hard can it be to control them? You're the adult. Show them who the boss is." And "Time, come on. You got summer off, plus all those vacations or long weekends during the school year. Who has an easier work schedule than a teacher?"

TODAY'S REALITY

In the following case studies, we will visit three classrooms. As with all portrayals in this book, the setting and the people in a case study are fictional, but the content of the case study is quite realistic. Case Studies 6.1 and 6.2 are presented as reflections from teachers about the classroom reality. Case Study 6.3 will take us into a classroom.

CASE STUDY 6.1

You asked me to put my thoughts, my ideas, my concerns, my frustrations on paper. That is a good suggestion that I do appreciate. I also appreciate the time you took to visit my classroom yesterday and then to meet with me after school. I know that your daily schedule as a high school principal is very demanding. Thanks for sharing your time.

It is very disappointing to me that I would seriously consider leaving the teaching profession. As with almost every new teacher, my first and second years were a collision of hopes, idealism, dreams, and the brutal reality of working in a classroom these days.

I really thought that the third year would be a lot better. I certainly have eliminated mistakes I made in the last two years. I use every idea that other teachers, the counselors, the academic team, and the administrators have given me. Still, in every class there are some absolutely incorrigible students. There are some students whose families make endless excuses, who blame me for everything, who complain to you and then to the superintendent about me, even though I have documented every action I took to help those students.

I assign homework and in some classes 20 percent of the students turn it in on time. We have a test, and some students expect me to provide their paper and pencil plus enough hints to make any answer obvious. How did those students get through elementary school and middle school? Were they just given D grades so they could move on? Did they fail so many times that it was strange to keep them with much younger students?

I assign textbook pages to read. The students do not take the book home to read it. So, we read pages out loud in class. Some students pay attention while others goof off or take a nap. I correct the misbehaviors and that lasts for a minute. I have used absolutely every reading strategy

I have been shown by the school district's reading specialist. The results are very limited.

I have used the word "rude" to describe student misbehavior. The students seem confused by the word "rude." Is that word new to them? Have they always been allowed to do and to say whatever they want to?

I arrive at school early to prepare the classroom and the materials. I stay at school late to grade papers and to copy materials for the next day. I thought that by not being the girls' soccer team assistant coach this year I would be able to keep up with everything better. I was wrong about that. I have one class with twenty-nine students in it, and nine of them have some condition that requires me to make individual accommodations for each of those nine students. Once each week another teacher comes to that class supposedly to monitor the progress of those nine students and to offer help to me as I work with those students. About every third week that other teacher is absent. When she is there my job is actually harder to do because she takes the nine students into the hallway one at a time for individual conferences. How productive can a class be with nine interruptions?

Speaking of interruptions and absences, there is never a day when all of my students are at school. They get behind, they do not make up work they missed, I remind them of the work they missed, I schedule time for them to come make up a test, and they do not show up. I call the families, I e-mail the families. I even mailed a test to one student, but he never completed it. What can I do when they do not attend school and when they refuse to make up work?

I do everything possible to improve their behavior. When necessary I write a discipline referral. You or the assistant principals have always taken action about each referral. The student returns to class and creates more problems. What does it take to get these persistent offenders placed in an alternative school? Do we really have to wait until they commit a felony before the powers that be will approve placement in an alternative school? And how does it make any sense for the parent or guardian to reject the decision of ten educators to place a student in an alternative school? A student who is court involved, who is repeatedly suspended, who is failing all classes obviously needs to go to an alternative school, but if the parent or guardian disagrees, the student stays here to commit more crimes, fail more classes, disrupt far more classrooms.

Despite all of this, I arrive early each day, and I stay late each night. I get my work done. If I have to change jobs, it will be with the peace of mind that I did everything humanly possible to make teaching work for the students and for me.

You asked me to tell you what I think could help. First, could we clean up the language that students use everywhere at school? When students think they can fill the halls, classrooms, cafeteria, office, library, and everywhere else with the ugliest possible language it is hard for anyone to do their best possible work.

Second, I've been through three professional development programs at this school. Those programs were in August, a week or two weeks before the school year began. Those programs were awful. Not one topic related to what I do in the classroom. Other teachers told me to just sit through the programs because we have to show that each year we are trained in some new concept. What a waste of time and money. What's wrong with taking those days as an opportunity for teachers to talk to each other? I'm sure our best teachers have some great ideas we could all benefit from, but we never have a chance to discuss ideas like that.

Third, the paperwork and the e-mail work are too much. Why does central office send us so much pointless e-mail, and why do they send so many forms, surveys, questionnaires? They need some procedure to limit what they send us and what they ask of us. The paperwork at school needs to be reduced, also. There is some form in my mailbox every other day. Can't somebody in the office screen those requests or take care of those forms?

There is a lot more I could say. Yes, some students try and some students cooperate. Some students make a real effort to learn. We have to find ways for teachers to give more willing and cooperative students more time and attention because they are more likely to respond to our efforts. The 10 percent of students who cause 90 percent of the problems have probably been causing problems throughout their education careers. They can be educated, but it takes a unique program at an alternative school. Those severe students gave up on regular school a long time ago. We can't give up on them, but we can't expect this one high school to be able to provide the perfect education for such a vast range of students from scholars to criminals. You know that I am telling you the blunt truth!

I should mention that my doctor asked me at my annual checkup last summer what I thought explained everything from some weight gain to increased blood pressure. Three years ago I was in perfect health. If teaching is going to wreck my health, I have to change jobs. I will follow your advice to improve anything I can do better. I'm beginning to think that one teacher just cannot sufficiently overcome the societal, educational, behavioral issues that are the reality of so many students. Something has to change, but that something is much bigger than one teacher or than what one teacher can do. I hope you can show me how to keep teaching. This is the work I prefer to do, but this is not the life I prefer to live.

Sincerely,

Mary Ellen Hunter

CASE STUDY 6.2

"Thank you very much for inviting me to speak to the regional association of school administrators. Throughout my teaching career of thirty-one years, I have taught in three different school districts, and all three of them are in the region of the state that your association serves. I have had the pleasure of working with some of you during the past thirty-one years. In fact, two of the people in this room hired me. Anthony Lawrence hired me twenty years ago to teach middle school English. Edward Harrod hired me ten years ago to teach high school English. So I am pleased to be with friends today.

"The subject that I was asked to talk to you about on this pleasant summer day in late June when we all have the time to assemble at this wonderful conference center that Central College made available to us free is time management for teachers. The assumption must be that since I have endured thirty-one years as a teacher, I must know something about managing time, or I would not have lasted thirty-one years and I would not be eagerly awaiting my thirty-second year of teaching.

"Before I share some time management ideas for teachers so you will have some more answers to questions your faculty members ask about time management, we have to begin with a realistic and accurate inven-

TODAY'S REALITY

tory of all of the demands that are placed on any conscientious teacher's time. Think, please, about every bit of work that a teacher is required to do in order to do the teaching job well. After everyone has thought for a few moments, we will make a long list of the many demands on a conscientious teacher's time. Keep thinking, please. Very good. You have had a few moments to think. Let's start at the very back of the room and just go across the rows to hear from everyone. Tell us one demand on a conscientious teacher's time."

- "Grading papers."
- "Taking attendance."
- "Planning lessons."
- "Phone calls to parents."
- "Phone calls from parents and guardians."
- "Attending faculty meetings."
- "Creating tests."
- "Grading homework projects."
- "Attending committee meetings."
- "Early morning duty."
- "Writing discipline referrals."
- "Writing letters of recommendation for students."
- "Attending special education meetings."
- "Going to professional development programs."
- "Entering every grade for each student on every assignment in the computer."
- "Answering e-mail."
- "Completing every form, survey, or other request for information from the state, the school district, or people in the school."
- "Creating makeup tests for students who were absent the day of the test."
- "Listening to students explain why they did not attend class or why they do not have the homework done or why they are late to class."
- "Having to answer the phone during class or deal with someone knocking on the door, interrupting class with some message from the office."
- "Completing curriculum and syllabus information requests."
- "After-school hallway or bus duty."

- "Attending the open house and other evening events during the school year."
- "Game duty to help supervise at athletic events."
- "Answering questions from the attendance clerk."
- "Teaching an extra class when a substitute teacher is not available or when another teacher has to leave unexpectedly."
- "Making copies of everything needed to distribute in the classroom."
- "Designing the classroom."
- "Preparing all materials needed for each class."
- "Setting up plans for a guest speaker, a field trip, a research project in the library or in the computer room."
- "Creating and grading final exams."
- "Representing the school at a meeting or on a committee arranged by the whole school district."
- "Talking to students informally before school, between classes, after school."
- "Doing reading and research to prepare for high quality instruction."
- "Keeping written documentation of every discipline action taken in the classroom and of every phone call or e-mail to families."

Katie Clinton smiled as she listened to these statements. She then continued her presentation. "That is a long list of well over thirty different tasks that teachers must do. We certainly could expand the list, but I hope that the overall idea is becoming very clear. Teaching is a more complex, more demanding, more time-consuming job today than it has ever been. The nation, our state, our school districts require teachers to accept additional duties, tasks, and responsibilities every year while all of the old duties, tasks, and responsibilities continue. That trend will continue.

"You may think that technology could help. Teachers enter every grade of every student into the computer. We also keep the old-fashioned paper and pen grade book record that is written by hand. Sure, the computer system can create very helpful reports or calculations, but for teachers, this doubles the time spent recording grades. The handwritten backup is essential to resolve any dispute or to protect against electronically lost data.

"So, in the category of time management ideas, actions, skills, or processes for teachers, what can be recommended? Through the years of my career, I have heard several major thoughts in this area, so I will share with you what teachers have told me for years, actually for decades.

"First, most professional development programs that teachers are required to attend are seen as a waste of time. That means they are also a waste of money. Imagine a faculty of one hundred teachers who earn an average of $200 per day. This faculty has to sit through an utterly pointless professional development presentation in August, a few days before the students return for the new school year. The wasted day cost $20,000 in wages. The wasted day cost eight hundred hours of time that could have been used productively with preparation for the school year. One way to help teachers manage time is to make professional development programs practical, realistic, and about topics that teachers indicate are important. Far too often professional development topics are chosen by people who are not teachers or are chosen to satisfy some political demand from within the education chain of command.

"Second, many other teachers and I agree that in the past few decades the trend has been for teachers to be told to do more nonteaching work. This includes monitoring hallways, keeping up written documentation of every contact with any family, going to more meetings before school starts in the morning or after school ends in the afternoon, completing all of the endless requests from central office for information so some bureaucratic report can be completed—this is especially frustrating when two or three requests occur in the same week or if they seem to be redundant—supervising after-school athletic events, monitoring students as they wait for buses after school, advising students on matters that they should see their school counselor about but each counselor has five hundred students to be responsible for so some of the students may not know their counselor at all.

"The point is, let teachers be teachers. Let teachers teach. Reduce the nonteaching tasks. It is impossible for a school counselor to really know five hundred students, so hire more school counselors. It is asking too much when teachers are told to supervise halls before school, during the school day between classes, after school, and when teachers are told to supervise at athletic events or in the bus-loading area. If the school needs more supervision, hire more supervisors. Teachers do their best work when they can concentrate on teaching. Do not balance the budget of the school district by getting each teacher to do the work of two people.

"Third, this may surprise you, but it is time. Teachers look at the annual school calendar and wonder how did those decisions get made? Our guess is that those decisions had a lot of input from people who do not work in classrooms as teachers.

"Look at the school year calendar. People wonder why school has to start in mid-August instead of the traditional late August or the very old tradition of the Tuesday after Labor Day. The calendar has the answer. Each year there are ten, eleven, or twelve days throughout the school year when we do not have school. Usually those days are on a Friday or a Monday, so that creates a four-day work week.

"Here's what teachers I have talked to say—a four-day work week does not result in 80 percent as much learning as would a five-day work week. Those four-day weeks signal to students that it is a time to coast through. Teachers are not fooled by these days off or these records days, conference days, semi-holidays, or just no-school days. We know that state laws require a certain number of school days each year, so the Friday off in October is a day added to May or August.

"Time would be more productive with more five-day school weeks. Let's be in school Monday through Friday more weeks than we are now.

"Here's another reason—attendance. I would think that attendance by teachers and by students is better on a Friday of a five-day work week than on any Thursday of a four-day work week when we do not have school on Friday. People stretch that Friday off into Thursday and Friday being off.

"Fourth, do not steal time from teachers. When the bell rings for class to begin, it is class time until the next bell rings to end class. Do not interrupt or disrupt that time. Do not call the classroom. Do not make public address announcements. Do not schedule activities that take students out of class. Set the example of good time management and set the standard that classroom time is precious. You do not interrupt football practices or marching band practices with phone calls or PA announcements, and the students know that. You don't schedule field trips during basketball practice or soccer games. Protect classroom time.

"The fifth and final point is for every new duty assigned to teachers by the national government, the state government, the local school district, or the school itself, an existing duty has to be removed. I count my hours each week. I manage my time precisely at school and at home. I'm experienced. I know every efficiency there is. I'm a good teacher. In all honesty, I am at capacity. Despite my desire to do the impossible, if I am asked to do more than I am currently doing, it will truly be impossible.

"Why are some teachers leaving this work after only a few years of teaching? The reasons vary, but a major reason I've heard from new teachers is that no matter how hard they work or how much they work, they can never catch up. Their friends in many other jobs work fewer hours per week for much more money. Their friends do not bring three hours of paperwork home to do each night.

"Let's consider that a teacher could have a total of 140 students in five classes during a day. If a test is given to all of those classes and it takes ten minutes to grade each test because there are two essay questions on the test because everyone says that students need to write more, that is fourteen hundred minutes of grading or over twenty-three hours of grading. When and where does that grading get done? What impact will that have on the family life of the teacher? How many other jobs on any given day could create twenty-three hours of take-home work? If the teacher is spending that time grading tests, when does the teacher create outstanding lessons for the students?

"The teacher could give a multiple choice test that a machine would grade. When would the students get experience with writing answers to complex essay questions? When would understanding, not mere recall, be tested? Do your teachers have friends in other professions who could talk of bringing home twenty-three hours of work to do?

"Their friends have secretaries, stock options, enough time for lunch, no hallways to supervise. For the future of this profession, it is absolutely essential that all of us seriously consider the increasing demands that have been placed on teachers, the toll that takes on teachers, the impact that has on students, teachers, and the education profession. Thank you for listening to me."

CASE STUDY 6.3

An eighth-grade social studies teacher offers a chronology of her workday on a Wednesday in October.

7:01 a.m. I really hoped to get here a few minutes earlier. I need to make a lot of copies. Well, I'll hope that both copy machines are working, that we have enough paper, that there is no line at the machines, and that there is nothing that I have to do unexpectedly.

7:14 a.m. Two minutes later, and I'd still be standing in line. By 7:03 a.m. three other teachers arrived behind me in the copy room. It took me thirteen minutes to copy everything I need for my six classes today and tomorrow. Some of the classes may move fast, so I had to complete everything for both days in case what I think will take all of today actually gets done faster in any class. At least the material I copied for the students is original. I hate to use the ordinary activities that textbook publishers provide for us. The time I spend designing material for my students looks like extra work for me, but when I design it the students learn better. Years ago I used some worksheets that came with the book, and I had students answer all of those predictable and ordinary questions at the end of each chapter. It kept the students busy, but that was all it did.

7:18 a.m. I have less than an hour. First-period class begins at 8:15 a.m., and students are allowed to come to the classroom areas at 8:05 a.m. I have to put a lot of grades into the computer. Wouldn't you know it? Fourteen e-mails. That will eat up much time. No. Not another meeting after school. Sorry for the short notice, but Ms. Lingate, you are requested to attend the meeting today after school of the Middle School to High School Transition Task Force. The good news is that the meeting is at our school. The bad news is that will be a long meeting, and two classes have writing tasks to do in class today, and I need to grade those today after school. Do the people who plan these meetings ever realize that teachers have teaching work to do?

7:41 a.m. So many grades to put in the computer. I started this twenty minutes ago and it will take five more minutes. I need to put some U.S. history vocabulary on the board. We have to save paper whenever possible. Those copies I made this morning put me at 50 percent or so of my copy allocation for October, and this is only October 10. I'll have to get the students to take notes more, and we have to do more with the overhead projector, but that projector machine is an instant signal to some students to get lazy.

7:46 a.m. Finally, the grades are finished. I have nineteen minutes before students will be in the classrooms. I have to write a letter to apply for that training program in gifted and talented education. I really want to attend that conference in June to learn more about gifted education. My letter is due October 15, so I'll get it done now. Who could be calling me on the phone? No, I cannot. I hate to tell another teacher that I cannot do their early duty, but this letter needs to be done. Supervising halls from 7:55 a.m. through 8:10 a.m. is a job for the administrators and the counselors, anyway. They don't have any grades to put in computers or instructional materials to make copies of, plus they have secretaries to help them. Whatever gets done for my students, I do myself.

8:10 a.m. That letter looks good. Hi, Thomas. Hello, Tasha and Shawn. Hi, Brandon. I hope all of you are ready for our Federalists and anti-Federalists debate. We'll start after the morning announcements.

8:12 a.m. Hello, hello. Jason, when's the next football game? Hi, Angela, does the academic team have a match this week? Hey, Jason and Jeremy, not so loud. Remember your first-grade teacher told you about indoor voices.

8:15 a.m. Everyone up for the Pledge of Allegiance. Good, now listen closely as you watch the morning televised announcements. I think two students from this class are reading the school news today. Yes, Rachael and Samantha are broadcasting. Listen closely to the announcements while I check attendance.

8:17 a.m. Open your notes to the list we made to summarize the major ideas of the Federalists and of the anti-Federalists. Take a minute to read those notes and to decide which of those two groups convinces you to agree with them. After our chosen Federalists and anti-Federalists complete their debate during today's class, we'll see if anyone thinks differently because of what you hear during the debate.

8:37 a.m. Now, you've heard what the Federalists and anti-Federalists thought. Great work with the debate. Everyone who debated really took us back in time to 1787 and 1788. Now, think of which side you agreed with before the debate and which side you agree with now. It might be the same side, or maybe the debate led you to change your mind. Write two or three paragraphs explaining which side you agree with now, the strongest reason for your agreement, and what you heard in the debate that confirmed your decision or that changed your decision.

8:38 a.m. Ms. Lingate, when is this due? Do we really have to write all of this? Can't we do something else?

8:38 a.m. That's a very interesting question. The answer is that yes, the writing is required and must be done right now. Also, I think you will see that what the Federalists and anti-Federalists disagreed over is still debated in elections today. After everyone finishes the writing, I'll show you six very modern television commercials from Democrats and Republicans. Even though we are more than 220 years past the writing of the U.S. Constitution, in some ways the Federalists and anti-Federalists debate continues.

8:39 a.m. But writing is no fun. Let's just watch the commercials.

8:39 a.m. Jennifer, it's like eating the vegetables before you eat dessert. Write now. Watch soon.

Ms. Lingate moved around the classroom to answer any questions, to prod reluctant writers, to encourage eager writers, to get some work out of Jennifer, and, much to Ms. Lingate's frustration, to confiscate Tony's cell phone when it sounded. Tony acted as if he were being separated from a life support system when he very angrily gave the phone to Ms. Lingate. This was a time-consuming chore that Ms. Lingate would prefer to avoid more than Tony would prefer to keep his phone, but Ms. Lingate knew that students had to see her enforce school rules or the rules would be of no benefit.

9:00 a.m. The writing was completed, and the commercials had been watched. The similarities and differences had been analyzed, the disagreements of Federalists and anti-Federalists, the disagreements of Democrats and Republicans, the issues of the 1787 era, and the issues of today were explored intellectually.

9:01 a.m. Please pardon this interruption. Some work is being done on the fire alarm system. If you hear the alarm, just stay where you are. Thank you.

9:02 a.m. Ms. Lingate stopped the chatter that followed the announcement. She completed class with a reminder of events scheduled for Thursday and Friday. She signed the daily monitoring sheet that seven students in this class use daily to provide their families with information about attendance, work, and behavior. The bell rang at 9:05 a.m. As the bell rang to end first-period class, the telephone rang also. The eighth-grade guidance counselor needed to see three of Ms. Lingate's second-period students about some potentially serious rumor they were allegedly spreading. The counselor would be at Ms. Lingate's room sometime during second-period class to get those students.

9:06 a.m. First-period-class students have exited. Second-period-class students are entering. This class begins at 9:10 a.m. and is also a U.S. history class. The topic is Federalists versus anti-Federalists, but the activity will not be a debate. Several of the students in this class are involved in the school's drama club, so they asked Ms. Lingate to let them write a play about the 1787–1788 debates over the new constitution. Today the play will be presented in class. The students who are not in the play will closely watch and then give reviews of the performance. The goal is for students to learn about the Federalists and the anti-Federalists. Ms. Lingate knows that applying the dramatic skills of nine students in the class can result in great learning for all of the twenty-seven students in the class. As the bell rings, the cast makes their final preparation, and right after Ms. Lingate checks attendance, it is showtime. Much to everyone's delight, Ms. Johnson, the assistant principal, has come to watch the play. Later in class when the counselor, Ms. Bell, comes to get the three students she needs to see, she quietly sits in the back of the classroom to watch the rest of the play.

9:28 a.m. That was magnificent. Yes, of course, everyone may applaud. That was a wonderful presentation. How about having our first reviews from Ms. Johnson and Ms. Bell.

9:31 a.m. After Ms. Johnson and Ms. Bell gave very favorable reviews of the performance, Ms. Bell took the three students into the hall with her. She used the idea of a play to solve the problem of spreading rumors. The three students played the roles of people whom other students were spreading rumors about. One of the students actually cried when she realized how much a rumor could hurt someone.

9:55 a.m. As second-period class ended, every student had written a review of the play after hearing the reviews from the audience. The review had to include evaluation of the performance and analysis of the competing ideas, the performance presented as Federalists and anti-Federalists argued on stage. Ms. Lingate would read all of these papers tonight along with the papers from her first-period class. That meant about two to three or four hours of grading papers this evening just for those two classes.

9:55 a.m. Second period ends with a bell signaling teachers to send their students to third-period class. Our attention now shifts to the principal's office where Federalists and anti-Federalists are not debating but where another type of debate has begun. The principal, Mr. Clay, is in a serious discussion with Ms. Chenault, a parent; Officer Wilmington, a school law enforcement officer; and Ms. Bell, the eighth-grade school counselor.

Ms. CHENAULT: They are picking on my son. Johnny almost refuses to come to school. He says that three other eighth graders bully him all the time, and they spread ugly rumors about Johnny. My boy is no angel, but he is a good student, and he stays out of trouble. These other three students will bully and tease Johnny one step too far, and I'm afraid somebody will get hurt. Johnny won't take this forever. He talked to a teacher who, I think, talked to Ms. Bell, but that's not enough. Do any of you know of any middle school bullies who are making good grades? These bullies pick on students and disrupt school. Please catch them, suspend them, have them arrested. I'll go from here to central office to complain, and then I'll go to the police. Actually, I already called central office and talked to Dr. Mitchell who is the supervisor or director or something of middle schools and high schools. He said I needed to meet with Mr. Clay, so I'm here. I really don't see why you let all of this bullying and teasing and making fun go on at this school. Can't the teachers control the students better than that? Isn't there some discipline action you can take? I'd say it's time I got some answers.

MR. CLAY: Ms. Chenault, I know Johnny. He is a good student, and we want school to continue to go well for him. This information from you is the first I've heard about anyone bullying or teasing Johnny. I see Johnny every day in the cafeteria at lunch, and he never said anything about it to me. Still, we need to investigate it thoroughly and deal with it completely. Does anyone have additional information?

MS. BELL: I just talked with three students from Ms. Lingate's second-period class. They admit that they have been involved in spreading rumors. They claim they did not start it, but they got involved and kept it going. Two of those students said Johnny was involved with them at first, but then Johnny quit spreading rumors because he realized it could get him in trouble. Apparently that's when the other three started bullying Johnny and teasing him. They said it had been going on for a week or so. When did Johnny tell you, Ms. Chenault?

MS. CHENAULT: He told me last night. I was so mad I called the police, and they told me to meet with school officials first. You're an officer. What can you do about this?

OFFICER WILMINGTON: The school law enforcement officers and the local police are two different organizations, but we work together when that is helpful. Our chief had an e-mail from the police about your call, and he sent that e-mail to me this morning. I was in court earlier this morning to testify against a student who had been arrested at a high school where I was helping for a week last month. When I got here this morning, I intended to talk to Mr. Clay and to Johnny, but when I got to the office you were already here. I'll do everything I can to help investigate.

MS. BELL: I had already planned to meet with Johnny this class period. I intend to get Johnny together with the other three students and fully resolve this. Officer Wilmington, your help in that meeting would be wonderful. Mr. Clay, is there anything else you would like us to do?

MR. CLAY: Yes, after you get to the bottom of this with all four students, tell me what you found out and include me in the final part of the meeting with the four students. Ms. Johnson is observing Ms. Lingate's second- and third-period classes today, so let's not interrupt her. Ms. Chenault, is there anything else you need us to do?

MS. CHENAULT: Call me when you get to the bottom of this. Keep an eye on Johnny this year, please. Maybe he did participate in the rumors at first, but he knows better. His father and I got divorced last summer and Johnny, well, it's rough on him. He may not always act like he used to, but I can't let him get in trouble and start making bad grades. So please watch out for him a little extra. Ms. Bell, maybe you could check on him some.

MS. BELL: I'll do that, and I'll see if he would like to get involved in a group of students who are from families where there has been a divorce. Sometimes it helps this age group to realize that they can relate to other people, that the problem they have is a problem that other people also have.

MR. CLAY: Ms. Chenault, you will hear from me by 3:00 p.m. this afternoon. Now, I need a favor from you. Please call Dr. Mitchell and tell him that you met with us and that you are satisfied with what we are doing. I want him to know that he does not have to come out here and deal with this himself.

MS. CHENAULT: I'll call him right after I leave. Thanks for helping. I wonder about these teenagers sometimes. Why are they so hateful to each other? Why all the bullying and teasing? I guess it's not easy to be a middle school student these days. Things have changed so much. I don't see how you do it. I don't see how you work with hundreds of these students every day.

MR. CLAY: We believe in the students, and we believe in what we do. We'll do all we can on this situation, and I'll call you this afternoon. Officer Wilmington, would you show Ms. Chenault out so she can find her way easily? Thank you.

While Mr. Clay, Ms. Bell, Officer Wilmington, and Ms. Chenault met, Ms. Lingate taught her third-period class. During the rest of third-period class and throughout most of fourth-period class, Ms. Bell and Officer Wilmington met with the four students and then with two more students whose names were mentioned often. The facts show that the six students had been teasing and bullying another student. Then Johnny tried to get out of the bullying activity, so the other five started teasing him. Mr. Clay was informed. All six students, including Johnny, were placed in the in-school suspension room for the rest of the day, plus they were given school service work to do. Their school service work would be to clean the cafeteria after lunch today and then to create a "no bullying, no teasing" commercial for the school's morning television news program to use tomorrow. The six students would also have Saturday detention, which meant being at school on Saturday from 8:00 a.m. through 11:00 a.m., reading for one hour, doing math for one hour, and writing an essay for one hour. The five students who teased Johnny were assigned to clean up the cafeteria tomorrow morning after breakfast serving ended at 8:10 a.m. Mr. Clay reported all of this information, without mentioning any names or any confidential information, to Ms. Chenault at 1:45 p.m., and she seemed to be satisfied. He would have called her earlier, but from 11:15 a.m. to 1:00 p.m., he monitored the cafeteria, making sure that 724 students and fifty-four teachers, counselors, staff members got through the lunch lines. At 1:10 p.m., he ate lunch quickly at his desk while also answering e-mails, including Dr. Mitchell's inquiry about Ms. Chenault's call to him. At 1:25 p.m. he stopped by Ms. Lingate's fifth-period class to see their Federalist versus anti-Federalist debate. Mr. Clay was very impressed with the quality work he saw the students do. Ms. Lingate has planning period during fourth hour. Mr. Clay monitored 778 people in the cafeteria during fourth period. He wondered occasionally if teachers realized what administrators do while teachers are in their classrooms. He also realized that the only planning period a principal has is early in the morning before anyone arrives or late in the afternoon after everyone else leaves. Either of those options makes a long, relentless day even longer.

1:50 p.m. The bell rang to signal to teachers that fifth-period class was over and they should send their students for sixth-period class. For Ms. Lingate, sixth- and seventh-period classes were unlike any other part of the day. During these two class periods, she has one group of twenty-five seventh-grade students for social studies and for English. It is an old scheduling idea that her school is trying because so many seventh graders have failed seventh grade in recent years. The hope is that one teacher working with one group of students across two class periods can build some relationships with the students, can be flexible with as much time as is needed each day on social studies and on English, and can get to know the strengths of the students as well as their academic problems so strengths are applied in ways to solve the problems.

The results so far were mixed. Ms. Lingate appreciated the flexibility in time. There were some days when both class periods were spent on social studies. One project involved research on the Egyptian pyramids using computers and books in the library, writing a report on the pyramids, and then using a variety of materials to make a model of a pyramid. Having the students in class from 1:55 p.m. when sixth period begins through the end of seventh period at 3:30 p.m. meant this activity could be completed from start to finish, which enabled students to better connect all the physical and academic parts of the project. Having these students during the final two class periods of the day sometimes challenged the students' endurance and Ms. Lingate's patience, but she was determined to lead everyone to success.

The most serious problems were that almost all of the students were behind grade level in reading, and almost all of the students had already failed a grade in school before reaching seventh grade. Some of these students would become fourteen years old during this school year. They were quickly putting themselves in the category of not likely to graduate from high school. Why? Because if they fail seventh or eighth grade, they would enter ninth grade at age sixteen and graduating four years later at age twenty was very unlikely.

The good news today was that right after school Ms. Lingate would meet with the school district's curriculum and instruction supervisor, Ryan Miller. They would be joined by Roberto Garcia, who taught science and mathematics to the same students during fourth and fifth periods. Mr. Miller had been an outstanding middle school and high school English teacher for nineteen years. He then worked as a drop-out prevention expert with one high school in the district for five years. His current work was based at the district's central office where he supervised K–12 curriculum and instruction, but he was in at least one school each day. Mr. Miller was the person in the school district to whom the school board directed very difficult questions at every school board meeting. The questions were about specific results from specific schools. One school board member often asked about efforts to reduce the rate of failure. That school board member was convinced that repeating a grade or repeating a class should never happen. Something should be done, she insisted, to intervene at the earliest sign that a student was not passing a grade or a class. Mr. Miller calmly and objectively answered every question, but he did wonder why anyone would be satisfied only with 100 percent perfection. Are any other parts of life perfect? Is that school board member required to be perfect in her work? Mr. Miller agreed with the goal of every student passing every grade and every class, yet he did not see how teachers and principals could guarantee such results given the many variables that impact student success. The schools can control some of those variables, not all of them. The meeting began at 3:35 p.m.

Ms. Lingate: Mr. Miller, it is so good to see you. Thanks for meeting with us today. Roberto and I talked some during our planning period today. We compiled all the data you requested in the e-mail you sent last week. So what topic would you like to discuss first?

Mr. Miller: Thanks so much for that extra work. You would be amazed how many times every day I am asked about the work both of you are doing. I get e-mails from school board members, from principals, from the state department of education, even from local members of the state legislature. There is so much concern about middle school students who get behind on reading, who fail a grade, who give up on school, and then eventually drop out of school. We are all convinced that great teachers given enough time and adequate resources can get more at-risk middle school students on the road to high school graduation.

I have great news. The state department of education has some grant money through a new federal government initiative. I applied for a grant. I had to go to Washington, D.C., to present our application in person because the funds are limited and because the grant manager at the U.S. Department of Education is required to actually meet with and keep in close contact with people whose school districts get the grant. I had to make four visits to the state department of education as applications were processed and as applicants were interviewed. The selection process was very thorough. I know that teachers sometimes wonder what those of us who work at the district office do all day. Well, all of the time, travel, and meetings to get this grant is one example of what we do. Our district was given a $25,000 grant. There are four other middle schools doing something like that at-risk work you are doing. Each school gets $4,000. Each of you will be given a $1,000 budget for instructional materials for the students in the group that meets with each of you twice daily. Also, every hour after school that both of you work together on this program will result in $25 for each of you up to a maximum of forty paid hours. The other $5,000 in the grant is intended for the teachers in the five middle schools involved in this Project Success plan to compile a how-to book showing other schools and other teachers how to implement this type of program. You would make presentations at a statewide conference and at a national conference, both of which are next July and both of which would be with your expenses paid. So, please update me on the Project Success program at your school.

Ms. Lingate: Roberto and I are finding out what works and what does not work. We have traded many ideas. He keeps me informed about the daily work in math and science. I keep him updated about our daily work in social studies and English. We have noticed that themes or overall topics are effective. Roberto worked with the students on how science and math were used to build the Egyptian pyramids. Then the students and I did historical research and writing about the pyramids. The four classes were linked with a common theme. I'm convinced that the students did quality work because they could build on what they learned in each class and apply that to the other classes.

Mr. Garcia: We have expanded that recently in two ways. First, our students in Project Success are taking a full-year computer skills and applications class. The computer teacher uses the topics from our classes. When the students saw the pyramids as an architectural presentation on the computer, they were fascinated. Now they all want to master computer design software for architects, engineers, and other jobs related to construction or manufacturing. Second, we connect with what students are already motivated by and committed to. Students love amusement parks. Their next math and science project is to create the "totally pyramid" amusement park ride. They can't wait to start.

Mr. Miller: Now that is wonderful to hear. I appreciate your work. What are the problems you are facing, and how can I help with those. Excuse me, that's my cell phone. Our superintendent is very interested in Project Success. He said he would call me during this meeting so he could talk to both of you.

Ms. Lingate and Mr. Garcia each spoke with the school district superintendent, Dr. William Fredricks, who impressed them with his knowledge of what they were doing. He promised that he would come visit their classes soon. He insisted that they e-mail him whenever he could be of help. With the phone conversations completed, Ms. Lingate and Mr. Garcia answered Mr. Miller's question about problems with Project Success.

Ms. Lingate: My biggest concern is attendance of these students at school. The overall school daily attendance rate is 93 percent. The students in this program have an average attendance of 77 percent. On the typical day five students in the Project Success class are absent. I need some help in getting these students to be at school much more consistently. The students who are doing the best work are the students with the best attendance.

Mr. Garcia: Here's the biggest problem I face. The students know they are behind. They know they have failed at least one grade already. They know they struggle with reading. So, they start asking me what can they do to catch up with their friends who never failed a grade and who are in eighth grade or ninth grade. I would love to have some way to give these students the chance to complete seventh and eighth grade during this school year. I think if they could actually be in ninth grade next year, they would do any work I tell them they have to do. I think we could make a contract with them that includes being at school at least 90 percent of the time so attendance improves. If Project Success is their ticket to high school next August, I think we would have a very amazing story to tell Dr. Fredricks, the school board, the state department of education, and educators everywhere.

Ms. Lingate: That's a great idea. Middle school can't offer these students a lot at this point except a creative way to catch up academically and then get to high school as soon as possible. Mr. Miller, can you help us with that?

Mr. Miller: I hope so. That's the type of creative thinking that Dr. Fredricks likes. There may be a bureaucratic maze to navigate through to get this seventh-grade-double-promotion-to-ninth-grade idea approved, but that's my job. You keep doing the great teaching. Put that grant money to good use for new instructional materials. Keep me updated on grades and other student achievement. I'll do the work at central office to get approval for this plan while you work with your principal and counselor to be sure they are supportive and that any concerns they have are resolved. I know that you have papers to grade and that you don't want to stay here all day, so I'll head back to central office. Thanks for the great work you are doing. I'll be back soon to observe classes.

4:10 p.m. Ms. Lingate has some preparation to do for tomorrow's classes, some e-mails to send, two families to call to report good news about A+ grades two students made on recent tests. She hopes to be on her way home by 5:00 p.m. She has two sets of papers to grade tonight and some reading to do for school, but from 5:00 p.m. through about 8:30 p.m. her time will belong to her husband and their twin seven-year-old daughters. Ten hours at school will have to be enough for today, but there will be two hours of schoolwork later tonight after the twins are asleep. Then tomorrow morning at 7:00 a.m., she will be back at school while her husband gets the twins to elementary school. The pace never slows down, but teaching is Ms. Lingate's chosen profession, and being wife and mother are her chosen personal joys.

In the three case studies presented in this chapter we visit today's reality in the classroom. For Mary Ellen Hunter the classroom reality has brought her to the point of probably ending her teaching career after only three years of teaching. Her principal is reaching out to offer help, support, encouragement, and ideas. Perhaps some actions can be taken that will address Ms. Hunter's concerns; however, she could conclude that even if her principal does everything possible to address her concerns, there will still be too many variables that cannot be quickly resolved or resolved at all. What can the principal do about court-involved sixteen-year-olds who do not take the legal system seriously to get them to take school seriously so they cooperate with Ms. Hunter? The principal is frustrated, just as Ms. Hunter is that some students who need to be placed in an alternative school sometimes are not accepted into such schools for reasons that are not logical or convincing. Still, the principal is reaching out to Ms. Hunter and will take every action within his authority and his jurisdiction to make it possible for Ms. Hunter to continue teaching. She is good at the work she does, but the work she does is not being sufficiently good to her.

The regional association of school administrators heard about the classroom reality from a very experienced teacher, Katie Clinton. She shared concerns about the many demands on teachers' time, the concerns and frustrations teachers have about anything that reduces instructional time, and the difficulties created for teachers when people who work outside of classrooms create more tasks for teachers to do. The fact that the administrators' association invited Ms. Clinton to speak to their group was encouraging to teachers who knew of Katie's presentation. At least people were willing to listen to what Ms. Clinton had to say about the classroom realities of too little time and too many demands being placed on that time.

The visit to Ms. Lingate's classroom also included a side trip to the principal's office and another trip to the school by a central office colleague. Ms. Lingate found that Mr. Miller was working hard for her at central office. She also was very encouraged that the school district's superintendent was aware of her Project Success work and was very supportive of that work. The principal, the curriculum and instruction expert, the superintendent showed ways to bridge the divides just as the assistant principal did by visiting Ms. Lingate's class. There is hope. The divides can be bridged.

The question for people who are not teachers is "Have you been in a classroom recently?" If yes, return often. If no, begin tomorrow, and then return often. No amount of information, reports, data, task force studies, think tank opinion papers, media editorials or news reports, political proposals, or interest group recommendations can replace personal knowledge of the classroom reality that comes from being there. Central office workers, school district superintendents, school board members, state education workers, state political leaders, and national political leaders cannot and need not spend all of their work hours in classrooms; however, they must spend some time in classrooms so the decisions they make, the policies they approve, the regulations they write, the laws they enact are based on reality. Unrealistic reforms of or changes in education typically fade away after the initial headlines are made and the subsequent opposition strengthens. Realistic reforms of or changes in education are based on the classroom reality; therefore, they have a better possibility of being effective, helpful, and supported.

Imagine a place where middle school and high school students like to spend time. Let's select a shopping mall. The owners of the mall have read reports about teenage obesity becoming a very serious problem. The mall institutes a new policy—before any persons aged thirteen to nineteen may shop in the mall, they must exercise for thirty minutes in the mall's new exercise facility. How would this new policy be enforced? What impact would this policy have on business at the mall? What happens when a family enters the mall and a friendly member of the Stop Teenage Obesity Police (STOP) force says, "The parents may shop but have to take your teenagers to the exercise room for thirty minutes of fitness training. They will be ready for you to get them in thirty minutes."

Teenagers go to malls so why not include malls in the nation's effort to stop teenage obesity? Teenage fitness is not the mall owner's responsibility. Mall reality is that shopping malls are efficient, enjoyable places to shop. Malls are not organized as places where teenage fitness plans are to be implemented.

Teenagers go to schools, so why not include schools in the nation's effort to stop teenage obesity by having each middle school teacher and each high school teacher supervise thirty minutes of exercise daily by every student? What impact would this have on the classroom reality? Unless the school day is extended thirty minutes, there would be a thirty-minute reduction in classroom instruction time. The classroom reality is that schools cannot be asked to solve every social problem that involves children and teenagers. Schools are not organized, staffed, financed, designed architecturally, or scheduled to be places where a fitness plan for each student is implemented.

But some celebrities, television stars, movie stars, and professional athletes testified in the state capitol before a state legislative committee asking those political leaders to get involved in the effort to make children and teenagers healthier. Those famous people were in the state for two hours and then went back to their lucrative work. If the state political leaders enact the law the celebrities endorsed, will the celebrities return and implement the new mandated fitness plan by going to every classroom in the state to help? No. Who is in those classrooms every day? Teachers. Listen to teachers so the classroom reality, not the celebrity excitement, is the basis of decisions.

Some societal realities, concerns, goals, problems, issues do impact parts of the classroom reality. Nonetheless, societal realities that are not addressed by academic instruction consistent with a school's curriculum should not be added to the current list of school responsibilities.

Many societal realities that can be addressed by academic instruction consistent with a potentially expanded curriculum of a school should not be added to the current list of school responsibilities because (1) other existing goals for school are more important, and (2) schools, as currently staffed, scheduled, organized, and financed, can accomplish good results toward a reasonable set of goals but cannot accomplish good results toward an unlimited set of goals.

Simply stated, schools cannot solve all personal, family, and societal problems that impact students. When schools concentrate precisely on causing learning via effective teaching, the results can be outstanding. When the school is asked to provide all possible social services while also creating academic success for each student, the result is competing goals, bureaucratic complexities, contradictory demands on resources, and mixed signals about the purpose of a school. Just to confirm, the purpose of a school is to cause learning. The purpose of a school is not to be our nation's one-stop processing center for every imaginable social service program for children and teenagers.

Classrooms can be places where there is abundant learning; however, the classroom reality is that causing learning is sufficiently difficult that diluting the attention that causes learning by simultaneously using schools to address nonacademic societal issues can reduce the possible academic achievement.

But, the critic contends, some of those societal issues could impact a student in ways that make it difficult for the student to succeed academically. "My child has gained so much weight recently. After her father and I got divorced, she just started eating and eating. Can you do anything to help us?" Educators are usually very caring people and sometimes are inclined to attempt heroic, messianic endeavors; however, beware. That mother and her ex-husband need to resolve the eating disorder their daughter has. A school counselor is not an expert in eating disorders. The school counselor could be helpful and supportive but does not have the professional certification or the job description of an eating-disorder specialist.

There is a hybrid solution. A school district and the many social services agencies in the community can increase their collaboration. The school district could have a partnership with a local hospital that has an expertise in childhood and adolescent eating disorders. The school counselor could connect the mother with this local hospital so the daughter can get the assistance she needs. This approach is caring, helpful, and efficient as experts get to do the work they are most skillful at doing.

In recent decades some students have brought with them to school an increased number of disorders, syndromes, juvenile justice records, family difficulties, emotional problems, anger issues, drug addictions, life-threatening habits, disease-causing practices, tendencies toward self-mutilation, consideration of or attempt of suicide, involvement with weapons, and other crises that did not exist a generation ago or existed only in much smaller numbers. All of these trends impact the classroom reality, but the classroom cannot be transformed into a full-service medical, psychological, societal clinic and still function as a place where academic learning is caused. Those many trends need solutions. Schools could be helpful members of unprecedented community partnership programs, but schools cannot be schools if in addition to being above all else, places where learning is caused, schools are asked to also be places where all societal issues involving five-year-olds through eighteen-year-olds are resolved.

Helping to create those new partnerships is an area where much help, leadership, communication, and management could come from school district central office workers and state department of education office workers in conjunction with other state social services colleagues.

Community leaders and interest group leaders could help. Teachers and school administrators must concentrate on their work at school. The growing need for a school and community social services partnership suggests an ideal opportunity for other people throughout the education universe to help organize these new cooperatives, partnerships, and networks. Of course, while doing this organization development work, communicate with teachers, administrators, counselors, and other people who work at schools. Listen to teachers. Dr. Earl Reum's words are eternally true: "People support what they help create."

In the intersection of societal issues, high stakes testing, increased school accountability, more demanding national and state laws about education, and more demanding school district goals for school performance is a teacher in a classroom. That teacher is the most important person and that classroom is the most important place in the process of causing learning for students at school. What can teachers do for themselves to take good care of heart, mind, body, and soul so they can thrive amid the classroom reality?

What renews the heart, mind, body, and soul will vary from teacher to teacher, yet several general ideas can apply to most people.

First, there comes a time in each school day—please note, this time must be after students are dismissed to leave school for the day—when you go home. Leaving school for the day does not mean that you are caught up with all school duties, that you have graded every paper, that lessons are perfectly planned for the next several days or weeks, that all phone calls have been made, or that all e-mails have been answered. You have completed everything that could not wait until tomorrow. You will grade some papers and prepare some lessons tonight at home. You could stay at school for more hours, but you have responsibilities to your family, your church, your friends, yourself, a group you do volunteer work for, so it is time to confidently leave school knowing you did a good job today and that you will eagerly return to do a good job tomorrow.

Second, treat yourself to a change of pace. At some point between leaving school and going to sleep, change the pace if only for a short time. Physical exercise, reading for pleasure, prayer, meditation, a walk, yard work, a hobby are possibilities.

Third, make every minute count with your family. Talk to each other. Have supper together. Share an activity.

Fourth, get enough sleep. You will be a better teacher tomorrow if you get sufficient sleep. You will be healthier also.

Fifth, there are many teachers in your school, in your school district, in your state, and throughout this county who are doing great work in their classrooms. You will rarely, if ever, visit those classrooms to observe that great teaching; however, you can trade ideas and success stories with those teachers. Create or participate in electronic idea sharing systems so when you are at home in the evening trying to create a perfect lesson you can efficiently read what other people have done. You will make the necessary changes in those ideas because you know your students and you know how your students learn, but just as physicians confer with each other about medical procedures that work, teachers can trade ideas about instructional activities that work.

This chapter asks the question "Have you been in a classroom recently?" to again emphasize the essential fact that all meaningful, effective, and practical improvement of education must be based upon the classroom reality.

Additional questions come to mind that relate to other locations in the education universe: "Have you been in a school district central office recently?" "Have you been at a school board meeting recently?" "Have you been in the state department of education office complex recently?" "Have you been in education committee meetings of the U.S. Senate or the U.S. House of Representatives recently?" "Have you been in the Oval Office at the White House recently?"

All of those places are busy. Some of those places are frantically busy. Urgent topics, vital decisions, life and death issues can occupy the attention of people in those places. No doubt, many people who work in those places experience difficulties and demands that can push the limits of endurance and of thought. For many reasons, including to help manage the workload of people in those places, when dealing with education begin with and emphasize the classroom reality. Presidents and governors care deeply about education. For that care to be translated into helpful action and for that care to avoid creating new problems, filter the care through the facts of the current classroom reality.

As the concluding thoughts on the classroom reality, encouraging words and blunt conclusions from some teachers will provide both hope and reality. The comments that follow were given to this survey question: "Despite the difficulties and the disappointments that teachers experience, despite the frustrations of teachers and the increasing demands placed on teachers, what motivates you to keep coming back to the classroom day after day, year after year?"

- "I love my students, and I think what I do for them is vital."
- "See students progress. Being able to use my talents to maybe make the world a little better."
- "The biggest parts of the job are still enjoyable. The pay is adequate for my lifestyle. The job is an important job. I'm good at what I do and I have the appreciation and support of my colleagues, students, and their parents."
- "Students."
- "I love the kids. They are so charming and fun, and when they learn—it's amazing."
- "Many teachers do not come back. I come back for my students and also because this job is a great schedule for me as a mom."
- "Honestly, I have sought other avenues due to the extreme demands and difficulties."
- "Getting hugs every day is a plus and just because I can make a difference in a life whether it is big or small."
- "I love the kids, especially those that are truly appreciative. Plus every day is different in this profession, which keeps the job interesting."
- "When my door is closed, with no administrator, parent, or test pulling me in another direction, it's the most stimulating and fulfilling thing that I could ever do."
- "The students, the students, the students. One kind note from a student, one invitation to a former student's graduation, one smile from a rascal."
- "I love my job and my students. I find it a challenge."

Having explored the classroom reality, the topic becomes what actions should be taken and what actions should not be taken. Those ideas are considered in the next chapter.

7

WHAT IS TO BE DONE?

Knowing what to do includes knowing what not to do. If a person needs to lose weight, knowing what to do could include more exercise, and knowing what not to do could include reducing or eliminating desserts to not eat those extra calories.

Knowing what to do about improving schools includes knowing what not to do. A failed education reform that never should have been tried in the first place can cause lasting damage. That failed reform can taint future innovation. That failed reform may have actually caused students, teachers, principals to spend time on unproductive activities—that time cannot be reimbursed, and the better experiences that should have happened during that time cannot be retroactively substituted. Because education impacts lives today and forever, inadequately considered changes in schools must be avoided.

Of all questions included in the survey that provided some ideas for this book, one question resulted in amazingly similar answers from many of the survey respondents. The question was "What gives you the most satisfaction or sense of accomplishment in your job as a teacher?" What prevailing thought is common to the following quote samples?

- "My rapport with the students—they give me 100 percent of what they have every day."
- "When a student gets the 'aha' look or says 'I loved that book we just read!'"
- "The relationship with students who feel comfortable enough to share problems that they may not share with anyone otherwise."
- "Working with a student who is difficult at the beginning of the year and turning him around is rewarding."
- "When a student says 'I get it' or a child tells me I'm the best teacher they ever had. Praise and encouragement from parents also give me satisfaction."
- "When my students' faces light up and you see they have reached that 'aha' moment."
- "When students try and succeed. I love watching them during tests and smile knowing they know it."
- "Students—working with them and knowing they are successful."
- "I love seeing young people grow and mature over the course of their high school career. I love seeing awe and wonder in their eyes as they learn something really different for the first time. I love establishing a positive rapport with all students."
- "Seeing students make progress. Knowing that parents feel their child has benefited from being in my class."
- "Seeing my students succeed at something they had been struggling with."

Those comments emphasize students and student achievement. For the teachers who wrote those comments and the many other teachers who would express similar thoughts, the greatest sources of job satisfaction come from interaction with students and causing learning by students. When student achievement is enhanced, the students benefit and the teachers experience the ultimate job satisfaction. That conclusion is not shocking, but it is a vital guide for anyone who would seek to improve schools. Do that which supports teachers in their efforts to cause learning, to enhance student achievement. Avoid anything that impedes the work teachers do to cause learning, to enhance student achievement. To learn more about what is to be done and what is not to be done, several case studies will provide details.

CASE STUDY 7.1

I have taught high school math classes for nine years. Before that I taught middle school science for three years. In college I had a double major in math and in chemistry. Right after college I entered a very accelerated three-semester program that enabled me to earn a master's degree and my teaching certification.

I do everything possible to improve my teaching each year. During each summer, I attend a conference about gifted and talented education. There is so much that is known about how to teach students who are identified as gifted and talented. Of course, some of those teaching ideas, actually most of those gifted and talented teaching ideas, can be applied in some creative ways to be helpful with almost all students. So, I always come back to school in August ready to use the most successful teaching methods I have seen work during my career as a teacher, plus I have new ideas from the most recent conference on gifted and talented education.

By the way, there is a huge amount of knowledge in the category of gifted and talented education. Books, websites, college professors, state associations for gifted and talented education, teachers, state-supported academies for gifted and talented high school students—there is just so much available to anyone who will take the time to read the books, to read the websites, to attend a conference, to join an association. The education profession has so many magnificent resources of ideas, of proven teaching methods that we do not need to guess or to wonder about what works. We know what works.

Well, then I return to school in August for the preparation week right before the students return. We usually have two or three days of professional development training and two days of faculty meetings plus time to prepare everything for the first day of school. The professional development days are dreadful, awful, atrocious. I'll admit that some of the teachers are impolite during those training sessions as they whisper, as they do paperwork, as they read the newspapers, as they send e-mails, or as they pay no attention. I resent that misbehavior. I also resent how pointless the professional development training usually is.

What makes that training so pointless? It is always, absolutely always, a series of spoken and video presentations about this year's new idea.

Can you see why I am so frustrated during those days of training? Someone who means well has hired someone else to come tell our faculty what another person or group thinks we need to know so we can do our job better. Who makes these decisions? Do they ever talk to teachers? Do they ever visit classrooms?

I'm not the only teacher who attends a great conference in the summer. I am always suspicious when teachers or school administrators go to conferences during January in California or Florida. Those events seem to be more about getting away from winter weather here than about finding great ideas. Why miss schooltime when you could attend a better conference in the summer and not miss school? For that matter, why go to any conference when so much information is available in books or on the Internet? The answer is because you can talk to people, interact with people, trade ideas with people, create ideas with people.

That is exactly what we do not do at our school's professional development sessions. We sit down, we listen, we take a much-needed break, we sit down, we listen less, we go to lunch, we sit down, we barely listen, and then finally we are liberated at the end of six ghastly hours.

What would happen if during those six hours we got to hear teachers on our faculty tell us about the most productive teaching activities they used last year with the students at this school? What would happen if we took some time, working with colleagues in our department, to create lessons that apply those great teaching activities from last year? We would have something that could actually be used to benefit our students and to create some great results. Is there anything wrong with that idea? Is it too simple? Does it not cost enough money? Is it rejected because unless professional development includes an expensive speaker from out of town it is not official?

Well, we survive those August days and then the school year starts. During the school year I am visited two or three times by an administrator who always tells me in our subsequent conferences how great a teacher I am. That is pleasing to hear, but when I ask for suggestions on what I could improve, I never get many ideas. The best idea came from the principal who years ago made arrangements for me to attend the state conference on gifted and talented education.

So, I've changed what I ask for in those post-observation conferences. I don't ask to be told what I could improve. I ask for names of teachers

WHAT IS TO BE DONE?

in this school whom I could learn from by visiting their classrooms. I also ask for information about great education organizations I could join or great conferences I could attend next summer. I also ask if the administrator has any information about outstanding books I need to read about teaching. My specific questions usually get much more exact answers than my other general questions about what I could do to improve. Maybe teachers just need to ask the right question to get a more helpful answer.

One other thought comes to mind that is different from professional development and classroom observations. Politics. That's right, politics. I realize that the money for public schools comes from the taxpayers so they deserve to be heard. The democratic political process includes the opportunity for every citizen to be heard. I've been to school board meetings and I've heard the public input. I'm fine with that. My concern is not the citizens who ask questions about the taxes that pay for public schools.

My concern with politics is actually twofold. One—all of those groups of people who think that the schools owe them something extra. The spokesperson for some group holds a press conference and makes endless accusations about how unfair the schools are to certain students and how some students are never given the chance to learn.

Get real. Any student who is willing to behave, listen, read, pay attention, do the homework, concentrate, think, organize their time, and ask questions will learn. I provide an equal opportunity for every student I teach. The group that holds the press conference spends more time trying to make headlines than they spend trying to help schools and students. I challenge those who complain about any unfair treatment or lack of opportunity to come into a school and show me a teacher who is not letting any student learn.

Two—politicians who seem to think that when they pass a law about schools the results they legislated will be automatic. They might as well pass a law that says every student is smart since they seem to think that we can make that happen, but we need them to make a law first. I've decided that it is much easier to pass laws than it is to get every student to pass every class.

What are the politicians thinking? I do not question their motive. I'm sure they seek improved schools. I question their judgment. Do they really think that all it takes is some long-awaited perfect law to be passed and then, finally, schools will be perfect? I just wish that the politicians would ask people in schools for ideas, for evaluation of existing laws or policies, for input. The politicians who promise the impossible need to come do my job for a few weeks. That would change their thinking and would make them so much more practical and respected.

So, my hope is that professional development should be much more practical, that schools should not have a new plan every year that is supposed to fix everything, and that politicians need to be more realistic. Am I asking too much?

CASE STUDY 7.2

Thank you for asking. I'll be glad to tell you what needs to be done to improve schools. Discipline. Discipline. Discipline. I teach seventh-grade social studies. Seventh grade means twelve-year-olds who become thirteen-year-olds. Some of them are wonderful people. Most of them cooperate most of the time. Then there's the other 5 percent or 10 percent. You come show me how to control them.

Do you realize that some of these thirteen-year-olds have been arrested, maybe more than once? From what I can tell, getting arrested has no impact on them. I talked to one of my students, and I asked him how he was going to finish middle school and graduate from high school if he kept getting arrested. Do you know what he said? I'll never forget his words. I think his words are the most tragic comment I've ever heard from a student. He said, "I won't live long enough to finish high school. The stuff I do, you know, it makes some people hate you, and then they finish you off."

Whatever crime he is involved in is so bad that he is convinced that someone is going to kill him. So, when he causes some problem in my class and I write a discipline referral, what punishment can the assistant principal give him that would work better than what a judge could give him?

Sometimes he has to be suspended from school—has to be because he brought drugs to school, assaulted another student, or vandalized part of the school. He probably wants to be suspended because then he has to miss school and because then he can do whatever crimes he does out in the community.

We had some training last August at our school about reaching the difficult student. I can reach the difficult students. I cannot reach the thirteen-year-old who is a repeat offender and a habitual criminal. I'm a teacher. That thirteen-year-old criminal needs to go to school in some institution that has never existed yet. It's a prison, a school, a vocational training center, a psychological counseling program, a detoxification center, a job training program, and a family therapy center.

The politicians who insist that every child should go to their neighborhood school and that every school has to somehow get through to every student are just plain out of touch with reality. Don't they know about specialties? Some hospitals have specialties in maternity wards or in treating heart attack patients. Some dentists specialize in cosmetic dentistry and others in dentures. Patients who need the specialized care need to go to the right hospital or the right dentist.

It's the same with school. There are some students today who resist every effort made by every person at a regular school. I would never give up on those students. I would realize that they need a completely different type of school to provide a completely different type of educational experience.

Then some group gets all worked up because 80 percent of students who get sent to the new educational facility are males. They claim some gender bias or discrimination. I resent that. I do not make up what I write on a discipline referral about the severe misbehavior of a student. Everyone is given an equal opportunity to learn in my classroom. Everyone is given an equal opportunity to avoid discipline referrals. I do not write fictional discipline referrals. I'd like to see those people who complain about bias come teach for a year. They would never last a year.

Discipline is not the only topic I need to tell you about. Paperwork. Paperwork. Paperwork. It's nuts. It's just plain crazy. Do you have any idea how much time the paperwork takes. Like the discipline referral, I have to write about that thirteen-year-old criminal. It's not just the discipline referral—I'll be asked to write a detailed incident report if it is possible that the student might face expulsion. So, that's an hour of paperwork. I don't have an extra hour. I have six classes to teach each day. I average twenty-six students per class. That adds up to 156 students.

How much paperwork is there for 156 students? Who does all of that paperwork? Do I have a secretary? See what I mean?

I know that the tests must be graded. I make myself get tests back to students no later than two days after they take the test. I really try to get them back the next day whenever possible because it is still fresh on their mind. I know that written assignments have to be graded. I know that my grade book has to be updated with the grades from each test or other assignment. I spend about fifteen to twenty hours each week on grading. It has to be done, and I do it well.

The paperwork that gets piled on top of the grading is what could be reduced or eliminated. "I know you are busy, but since your school participates in the federal and state government partnership for high school readiness initiative, we need you to complete the twenty-five questions, please. Just return this via e-mail by Friday of this week. The short notice could not be avoided."

On the same day, we get other e-mail saying, "The school district has been told by the state department of education that because of a complaint filed recently, it will be necessary for each teacher in the middle schools to keep written records of every academic reward given to students and of every discipline action taken by teachers that did not result in a discipline referral. Apparently an allegation of discrimination has been registered so this documentation is needed. You will submit information each Friday for the rest of the school year." One allegation, valid or not, justified or not, based on one person's genuine concern or maybe based on one person's animosity, results in all of this paperwork. Paperwork done electronically still takes the time that paperwork takes.

Then we get endless requests for forms to be filled out by our school counselors, our school administrators, the social worker who comes to our school two days a week, the special education teachers, the drop-out prevention program director, the at-risk students program supervisor, the PTA, the athletic program/activities manager, the cafeteria manager, the librarian, and more. All of those tasks consume time that should be spent on teaching. Somebody in the state department of education and in each school district should create a paperwork reduction project. Each school should create a simplified, efficient, and limited system for obtaining information from the faculty and staff. Everything teachers are asked to do that is not teaching takes away from teaching.

One more topic needs to be mentioned. This is something that only a teacher would say. Schools do a lot to help students who make bad grades. There are second chance programs, remedial programs, summer school, programs with computer-based classes that give you the chance to make up what you failed last year, before-school tutoring, after-school homework help, and much more. We need to keep doing that, but we do not need to add more programs for the students who struggle. They are being given enough second chances, and they just need to do their part to make it work.

What we do need to add is more opportunities for two groups of students. One group is stuck in the middle with C averages. They never fail a class. They never make an A in a class. They make a rare D or B grade, but somehow they have become experts in making C grade after C grade. Those students will probably have a better chance of going from C to B with a little extra effort on our part than an F student would have of moving up to passing if we added another program directed to students who fail.

One other group deserves new opportunities and new challenges—the honor roll students, especially those for whom school is really easy. Let's be honest; a bright student who does the required work in middle school will easily make A and B grades but has the ability to do much more difficult work and would prefer to do more difficult, more interesting, more challenging, more meaningful work than is common in the middle school curriculum. Don't pass some crazy, complex, complicated national or state law about this. Solve this problem at the school level. Come on, middle school teachers and administrators, take the lead on this. You know that some of your students can do much more than what the typical, generic, one-size-fits-all curriculum includes. You probably have some teachers with the certification and the eagerness to teach a more demanding class, so apply their talents in ways that enhance their careers and that provide new opportunities for your most capable students.

Here's my conclusion. School is about people. What I love best about being a teacher is that I get to be for my students what my best teachers were for me. I do this work to inspire students, to challenge students, to encourage students, to guide students, to help students avoid mistakes, to make students aware of what they can achieve now and of what they can become. I'm in the classroom for the students, those amazing people who bring with them each day a new problem, yet a new potential.

The proper emphasis in education is students. We are here for students. Sometimes, the best actions that can be taken for students are the actions that do the most good for teachers. We are the people who work directly with students. So, if the people who make the decisions about schools would think of teachers more and listen to teachers more, those would be among the very best ways to do the most good for students. School is all about students, and school is always about students. That's the right priority. What better way to serve students than to provide the best possible support for, help to, guidance for, sensitivity to, appreciation of, understanding of the teachers who are the people who, more than anyone else in the whole education system, will determine the quality of the learning experience of students.

CASE STUDY 7.3

I teach fifth grade. I have taught other grades in elementary school, but I'm really intrigued with fifth graders for now. I have been an elementary school teacher for twenty-three years. I hope to keep teaching for ten years, although sometimes I think about becoming an elementary school principal. I would miss teaching, but some of my concerns about school are beyond what a teacher can do. Here's what I mean.

When I started teaching, it was common for the mother and the father to come with their child to school on the night of open house. Now it seems more common for the child to live with only one parent or for the child to live with an aunt or a grandparent. Sometimes a child moves from aunt to grandparent to adult sibling back to parent. Family situations can be so different now.

I think that means we need a full-time school social worker who keeps in touch closely with families so we know where a student is living now, whom to contact about the student, and if anything is changing. I'm certainly not saying that the school needs to become the support system for the family. I'm saying that for the school to be a school we need to staff our organization so teachers can teach and other staff members can apply their expertise to these new situations. If a student is struggling and a teacher cannot get a family member on the phone or cannot get a response to a letter or cannot get the family member to attend a meeting at school, we need an expert in situations like that to help out. The trend is growing. More and more students live in different family arrangements, such as being reared by a grandparent. Bless their hearts, the grandparents tell us how complicated it can be to take care of their ten-year-old grandchild who never knew her father and never sees her mother. The social worker could help that grandparent arrange for support from various community agencies and could be a communication link with the school. That would provide more time for teachers to be teachers.

Similar to that, have you seen how much medicine is kept in the offices at schools for students to take every day? What is going on? This is the most medicated group of children I have ever seen. It was not like that twenty-three years ago when I started teaching. Families took care of medication for children then. Now, some state law says school must manage, control, keep records, dispense medications to any student whose family makes an official doctor-approved request. Of course, the state law provided no training to show the school staff how to become pharmacists and provided no funds to pay for this extra duty. Imagine the liability involved with having all of those medications at school. Why are so many children taking such powerful medications? Why is the school supposed to manage this? How can I teach students who really have the conditions that these medications are prescribed for?

That's one more example of how society has changed in the past twenty or thirty years. Maybe some of these children do benefit a lot from the new medications. Maybe parents and guardians are hoping that medicine will do what good old-fashioned strict parenting used to do. Here's what I know—schools are expected to manage all of these medications with the precision of a pharmacy. Are we given more staff to do this? No. Are we given liability insurance in case, heaven forbid, some mistake was made or some schedule was missed with medication for a student? No. Schools are asked to do too many things that schools just are not organized to do or just plain are not supposed to do. Who makes sure that these students take their medications on weekends or in the summer? I've heard our principal say that she got a call at home on a Saturday morning from a parent who expected the principal to go up to the school and meet her there so she could get her child's medicine since she did not have any at home. At least she knew the child needed it, but is that what a principal is expected to do on Saturday morning?

Here's my big idea. I would like to see my school completely evaluate everything we do. Some of the classes we teach, some of the teaching methods we use, some of the procedures we follow are very effective; however, some are terrible and get continued just because we have always done it that way.

My hope is that we keep doing what works best and we quit doing what does not work at all or what works very poorly. Then, we ask every teacher to make one suggestion. We take the best suggestions and we implement those. We would expect teachers to offer suggestions that they know are superior based on what they learned in a graduate school class they took recently, based on a great book they read, based on what gets the best results in their classroom, based on conversations they had at a conference when teachers told about classroom success stories.

Then, for several years we completely and correctly implement those carefully selected new ideas and we keep using the best parts of what had been working. We do not change directions every year. We take the time to fully and effectively implement the best of the best ideas. Sure, teachers would make adjustments as they go based on what they learn about the needs of or the strengths of their students. We would avoid the dreaded "new idea for the year" speech given in August by the principal who knows that we never finished implementing or evaluating last year's new idea for the year.

Notice, the national government would stay out of our school's plan to create our own future. The state government's job would be to tell us where we can get information about teaching ideas that are working best in elementary schools throughout this state. The school district would send people to visit our classrooms to help us evaluate how we are doing and to offer perspective on what we could consider adjusting to improve.

I do have one more concern. When you ask me what I think needs to be done to improve schools, I think of those college students who today are thinking about becoming teachers. Based on all of the societal and educational trends I have seen impacting schools during my career, can

I honestly recommend teaching to someone who would be doing this work during the next thirty or thirty-five years? Can you imagine what they will have to deal with during that time?

For college students who are convinced that their purpose in life is to teach, yes, come teach because if you are cut out for this work, nothing else will satisfy you even with the frustrations and difficulties you will face. If life tells you to work with students, then you have to be where the students are.

If you have a religious conviction that God has given you the talent to teach, the heart to be a teacher, then accept that holy calling and come teach. Hold on to your faith as a source of strength in the most demanding moments of your career in the classroom.

If your goal is to make a lot of money, that will not happen in education. If your goal is to be famous, look elsewhere. If you seek stock options and profit sharing, school is not the place for you.

If you just see teaching as a plan B in case your plan A does not work, think again. You do not succeed in teaching if you give it a plan B commitment.

So, our profession needs to think about what we can do to attract great college students to make a serious commitment to teaching as the profession of teaching makes a serious commitment to those great college students.

Our profession could face a teacher shortage soon. My son is a lawyer. He finished law school two years ago. I've been a teacher for twenty-three years. My son makes more money than I do, actually about 50 percent more. He and I added up the hours we each work in a year. He averages sixty to sixty-two hours per week for fifty weeks a year. I average seventy hours per week for forty weeks a year, and in the summer, during spring vacation and during Christmas vacation, I average ten hours of schoolwork per week. The totals are 3,050 hours per year for my son at an average of 61 hours per week and 2,920 hours per year for me. He works 4 percent to 5 percent more hours and makes 50 percent more money.

My daughter majored in Spanish in college. High schools need Spanish teachers, and she considered a fifth-year program to earn her teaching certification, but three large banks recruited at her college in search of students who were bilingual. She had three very attractive job offers, and the office where she works is as different as you can imagine from what a school is like. My daughter's starting salary is not much more than a teacher's starting salary, but the working conditions appealed to her, and all of the benefits provided by her employer were generous.

So I am concerned that schools just are not very attractive places to work for people who do not have an absolutely compelling dedication to be a teacher no matter what the pay is or what the working conditions are.

CASE STUDY 7.4

I retired from teaching two years ago. I taught for thirty-three years. There were some financial incentives to stay until I was fifty-five years old, so I did that. I could have retired after thirty years, but I really like teaching and that financial incentive certainly improved my retirement benefits.

I'm asked from time to time what I think needs to be done to improve schools. There are a lot of answers I could give, but there is one that stands out. About fifteen years ago state departments of education became obsessed with annual tests that had to be given to all students or almost all students in all schools. From that time on we heard more about test scores and the detailed data within those test scores than we heard about anything else in the schools, including students and learning.

It never bothered me to teach to a test. In fact, that is rather logical. When I gave my students a test it certainly related very directly to what we had been studying.

It did bother me that those annual tests were emphasized so much. We took a week in April or May and gave students about seven or eight hours' worth of tests. Imagine if I taught a high school class and the only thing that counted for a grade was a test students took in May. Nothing from August through April counted toward their grade. Would that make any sense? These annual tests create stacks of reports with endless statistics, numbers, charts, and other data. People analyze all of the data and reach some urgent conclusions that are supposed to be the basis for everything we do to get our test scores up.

Wait a minute. I was a teacher—not a data analyst. I taught students—not data. All of those reports, charts, data from the test analyses never told me anything about a student. Our school's reading score went up one year and then went down the next year according to the test data. Who was reading better and why? Who was reading worse and why?

The national government and the state government seem to think school is all about test scores. Well, is the national government passing the test of protecting the borders of this country or of balancing the government's budget? No, but they insist that we reach our test score goals and requirements.

I would suggest that the national government remove itself from any role in testing in K–12 education. Education is not a national government duty. It is complicated enough for school administrators and teachers to keep up with all of the test requirements that the state government requires.

Schools are about students. I could tell you how any student of mine was doing in every class I taught. I could tell you more about my students than any national or state test could tell you. I think that is true for most teachers. If you need to know how students are doing just ask their teachers. The teachers are with the students every day of the school year. Ask the teachers. Nobody knows the students as students better than teachers do. One minute of information from a teacher about a student or students is better than one national or state set of numbers.

If the current testing obsession continues, schools will do little more than drill students for the annual tests. There is so much more to learning than those tests can measure. There is so much about being a great student or being a great school that the data cannot measure or reveal. Let's not reduce students to a test score. Let's not reduce school to a set of data. Let's not reduce teaching to a perpetual statistical analysis.

Now. Let's take time for the reader to think about what is to be done to improve schools. What is on your list?

1.
2.
3.
4.
5.

Now, eliminate one of those five ideas because the other four ideas could have more impact. Then get the list down to three. Evaluate those three in terms of the classroom reality. Will these ideas help teachers cause learning? Will these ideas impose impractical time demands on people who already have too little time? How will these ideas make the teaching experience more rewarding to the teacher and the learning experience more meaningful and productive for students? Do these ideas really pass through the classroom reality filter or would these ideas add to the paperwork, the bureaucracy, the non-educational tasks, the political interference, the competing goals that already exist within the education universe?

There is no end to the possible answers to the question "What is to be done to improve schools?" Those answers can be divided into two groups: (1) ideas that are practical, helpful, and can benefit teachers as they work with students, and (2) ideas that complicate the classroom, that are counterproductive for teachers and students.

How are the two groups chosen? How can an idea be assigned accurately to the correct group? Listen to teachers. Teachers live the classroom reality daily. No other adult involved in education, concerned about education, or seeking to impact education lives the classroom reality all day, every day. Many people need to be heard in the overall discussion about improving schools; however, there is much about education that only teachers know. Real improvement of education requires an understanding of the classroom reality. Where is that understanding found? Who can provide the information needed for that understanding? How can the classroom reality be understood by people who do not work in classrooms?

Listen to teachers. This means that teachers need to politely, diplomatically, repeatedly, persistently tell other people about the classroom reality. Keep the principal and the assistant principal informed. Serve on committees in your school, in your school district, and in your community, talk to school board members, talk to and e-mail central office workers in your school district, volunteer to be involved with school improvement efforts. For other people to be able to listen to teachers, teachers need to take the initiative to speak up.

Write articles for your school's website and your school district's website. Have your own webpage all about your classroom.

Write articles for the PTA newsletter and for publications of other groups in your school, your school district, your community.

Write articles for education publications in your state and in the nation. Each state has many professional organizations of educators, and their publications need your ideas.

Some neighborhoods have publications that seek articles. Some newspapers welcome guest columnists, some radio or television stations welcome guest commentary.

Seek opportunities.

Faculty lounge gossip does not help. Generic complaints expressed around the copy machine do not count. Wisely directed, professionally chosen words do count. Speak up, remembering that not every thought that comes into the brain should come out of the mouth. Think, edit, speak. Teachers who speak that way are teachers who are listened to more often and more seriously. Be true to your convictions, but be aware of your audience and how you are perceived. What you say is half of the communication process. How you say it is the other half of the communication process. Be wise about both halves and the process of listening to teachers will increase in productivity.

The final pages of this book will include professional insights in chapter 8 plus thoughts and feelings of a personal nature in the epilogue.

8

LESSONS LEARNED

Five months later and I still cry. When I think of the death of the student to whom this book is dedicated, I shed new tears. When I think of the vibrant, inspiring, original, creative, meaningful life that Murphy Jones lived, I give thanks that I had the honor, the joy, the privilege, the gift of being his teacher. This book is dedicated to Murphy.

Part of what teachers know is that teaching can nourish your soul and break your heart. Teaching can renew your mind and exhaust your body.

To truly, accurately, and realistically know what is occurring in schools today, what is working in schools today, and what is needed in schools today, input from teachers is essential. Additional input is also important; however, any input that is not from the classroom has a less direct connection to the classroom reality than does the input from teachers. Some people could have questions about or concerns about tilting input too much toward the teacher perspective. That issue merits further consideration.

CASE STUDY 8.1

PRINCIPAL: I've been doing this job for ten years. Before that I was an assistant principal for five years and a teacher before that for eleven years. That's twenty-six years in this education business. I have no thought of retiring. Why stop working now when I know more about school than I ever knew. The lessons I have learned in my twenty-six years should not evaporate with retirement. More lessons learned need to be applied.

ASSISTANT PRINCIPAL: Of course, I'm still new to school administration. Working at this school with you got my school administration career off to a great start. I'm envious about all of those lessons you have learned. From working with you for one year, I certainly learned the importance of getting out of the office and into the classrooms, hallways, cafeteria, everywhere that school really happens. I learned to do the paperwork early in the day before students and teachers arrive or late in the day after dismissal. I learned to know the policies of the school district and the school so I always follow the policies. I learned to acknowledge good work done by students, teachers, and staff. I learned that a few teachers do great work, many do good work, a few do acceptable work. Then there is a very small number of teachers who are just not doing the job even though they claim that the daily routine of textbook, worksheet, and video is perfectly legal. I learned that the teachers who used that textbook, worksheet, and video routine over and over wrote the most discipline referrals and had the most complaints about everything.

PRINCIPAL: I hope that you also learned from me that we have to listen to all of the teachers and all of the staff members. I know that we have some chronic complainers who look at every possible person, policy, or budget to blame for problems at school but who never look in the mirror and think that the person in the mirror could be part of the problem and must become part of the solution.

ASSISTANT PRINCIPAL: I know you are giving great advice. I just get so tired of listening to the endless complaints of people whose goal each day seems to be to complain.

PRINCIPAL: The principal I worked with when I began my assistant principal job told me that listening to people who always complain is the price we pay to talk with them about what we need them to hear or to do. She also told me that sometimes within the perpetual complaints could be a real concern that needs to be addressed. So, I promised myself to be a school administrator who makes the extra effort to listen to people.

ASSISTANT PRINCIPAL: Doesn't that take a lot of time? There are people who would talk to us all day if we would sit in the office and listen for hours.

PRINCIPAL: Good point. I prefer to keep moving. I minimize my time in the office during the school day. When I am in the classrooms, in the hallways, in the cafeteria, in the teachers' workroom, or at school events after school dismisses for the day, I have a lot of short conversations with many people. It is rare that people ask if I have time to talk with them or ask if they could schedule a time to meet with me. I always suggest right now as the best time to talk. Sure, if someone needs to meet with me in the office away from the crowd and the usual activity, we make those arrangements. I have learned that dozens or hundreds of short conversations every day with teachers, staff, and students help you keep up with the pulse of the school. People can always follow up with an e-mail. Sometimes I'll send an e-mail to confirm what a teacher and I agreed to or to give some information I had to go look up. E-mail is fast, efficient, and helpful, but it does not replace face-to-face listening and communication.

ASSISTANT PRINCIPAL: What do you do when you listen to ten teachers about a certain topic and five teachers support an idea while the other five teachers oppose the idea? Where does listening take you then?

PRINCIPAL: It's lonely at the top, isn't it? I don't listen with the expectation of hearing identical ideas from everyone. People appreciate being listened to, being heard. As you know, the school has a governing council and a committee system, so that formal decision-making process is known to everyone. If it is a decision that is mine alone to make, I listen to all available input. I obtain all applicable information. I review the goals of the school, and I select the option that most effectively advances us toward those goals. Well, we better get back to the second half of today's administration training. It's great to have time like this in the summer to talk during lunch.

ASSISTANT PRINCIPAL: Let's do this again soon. I'm really interested in the afternoon sessions about what has been most effective at schools in our district to get creative with discipline actions. That one school that reduced suspensions by 50 percent with a Saturday work/study plan may have some ideas we could borrow. Some teachers at that school created the program, got some budget flexibility approved to pay faculty members to work on Saturday mornings, and are convinced that the plan is working.

PRINCIPAL: Let's go. We want to listen to everything those teachers can tell us. Listen. Listen more. Keep listening.

CASE STUDY 8.2

RETIRED TEACHER: I taught for thirty-two years. I retired four years ago. Now I substitute two or three days each week. It's a good schedule for me. My name is Susan Altwood.

NEW TEACHER: Hi. I'm Brittany Findley. This is my first year of teaching. I'm really glad to meet you. Our principal told us that you taught at this school for a long time and that you visit with the new teachers every August before the school year starts. I'd really like to hear about what has changed in teaching since you started and, you know, what is not different at all.

SUSAN: That is part of what I'll share with all of the new teachers. I'll give you a preview. Deep down inside, today's students have a lot in common with the students I taught throughout my career. Society has changed. Families have changed. Laws about education change all the time, probably too much. I think that students thirty years ago and students today respond to a teacher who takes the time to get to know the student, who creates learning activities that are lively and interactive whenever possible, who builds on interests that students have. I always remember my student who loved computers. He will own a computer company someday. The problem was he hated to write, and I had to teach him about writing. When the school upgraded computers, I got one of the old ones for him to take apart and put back together. He loved that. He had to write an instruction book about how to assemble a computer. His book was masterful. He could write as well as anyone from that point on.

BRITTANY: I have so many other questions I would like to ask, but it looks like everyone is here so I'll sit down and listen. Thanks for talking to me, and thanks for being here.

SUSAN: Good morning. Your principal is very busy this morning as new students are coming to register for school and as some unexpected interviews are held. One of the teachers just became an assistant principal at a nearby school, so that means a teaching position needs to be filled. I told your principal to get his work done, and we would be fine. I'm Susan Altwood. I taught elementary school and middle school for a total of thirty-two years. I retired four years ago, but I stay involved as a substitute teacher. I'll share some thoughts with you about what I learned during those three decades of teaching. I hope that my experiences and my lessons learned will be helpful. First, please introduce yourselves. Tell us your name, what you teach, and something important about why you became a teacher.

HANNA: My name is Hanna Barnes. I'll teach sixth and seventh graders who receive special education services. I became a teacher because I had some great teachers, and I always wanted to be like those teachers.

CATHERINE: I'm Catherine Reynolds. I'll teach sixth-, seventh-, and eighth-grade Spanish classes. I became a teacher because international languages fascinate me. I hope that my students will get excited about learning Spanish.

KYLE: My name is Kyle Anderson. I get to teach seventh-grade math. I'll also coach the boy's basketball team. I became a teacher because when I was in middle school and high school I had two great basketball coaches. I promised myself that I would coach my teams the same way those great coaches coached my team.

REGINALD: My name is Reginald Williamson. I teach eighth-grade science. I'll admit that I teach because I really believe that a lot of students fall through the cracks, they get overlooked, they pass, but they could do much more. I want to reach out to those students who don't have many people or anybody advocating for them.

ELIZABETH: I'm Elizabeth Columbia. I'll teach sixth-grade English classes. I became a teacher because I thought it would be a good job after my husband and I have children. I want to be a good teacher, but I want to be a great wife and mother. The teaching schedule will fit in well with taking care of my children.

SUSAN: Kyle, I'm glad you mentioned coaching. Here's my request—expect more, demand more of your students in the classroom than you do of your students at basketball practices. Be a great coach. Be a greater teacher. We usually get very impressive work from the athletes in their sports. We know how to get the best effort from students in sports. We have to get even better work from students in classrooms.

Now, what are the topics for us today? First, some thoughts on what has changed and what has not changed in teaching during the past thirty years or so. Second, some survival tips so you take good care of yourself. Third, a few ideas about what makes the job of teaching unlike any other job.

What has changed in the past thirty or forty years about teaching and about school? I think that what has changed the most are those things we can't do anything about. So, concentrate on what you can impact. Society has changed. You and I cannot change society. We certainly do have to contend with the impact of societal changes. For example, one of your students lives with his mother and stepfather. The father and stepmother also live here in town, but the father has been in jail for almost a year. He will be released from jail in a month. There is an older brother who has been arrested twice for driving under the influence of alcohol. There is an older sister who has a three-year-old daughter, but the sister has never been married. The sister and her daughter live in the same house as the mother, stepfather, the older brother, and your student. There were no students whom I taught thirty years ago in living circumstances like that, but the student deserves the very best teaching you can provide. In fact, you could be the most important teacher the child ever has.

Here's an editorial. It will be very frustrating when you have politicians talking about everything they are going to do for schools. Those politicians usually mean well, but they rarely are fully aware of the circumstances your students live in or of the circumstances you teach in at school. If you find an opportunity to inform those political people about what school is really like, more power to you, but concentrate your efforts on teaching. The one part of your career that you can control is what you do in your classroom and how you do that in your classroom. Even if what you teach and how you teach have to fit certain requirements, the personal interaction, the enthusiasm, the atmosphere in your classroom are all up to you.

Never spend any time wondering what you should do, worrying about how to create a better lesson, wishing there was some material you could use in your classroom, or yelling at the computer when it rejects the attendance or grade information you are trying to enter. Ask someone. Talk to another teacher. Ask the principal, the assistant principal, the school social worker, a school counselor, another teacher. You are surrounded by experienced people who are good educators. Get their ideas, their advice, their help. There is no reason for you to struggle in isolation.

Tests are everywhere. Thirty years ago my students took a few standardized achievement tests. The results helped us evaluate each student individually. Now schools have to spend so much time with students taking tests for the local school district, for the state department of education, or for the national government.

Go ahead and teach to the tests as part of what you do. Kyle, you coach to the game, right. You coach your athletes so they can do well in a game, which is like a test, but you coach them to master some skills or traits that the basketball scoreboard does not measure. To the extent that the topics on these new, all important tests are known, absolutely make sure that your students are test ready, but teach them a lot more math, science, social studies, or English than the tests include and measure.

One more topic before we take time for your questions. Teaching, if done correctly, is inspiring and is exhausting. Be good to yourself. Do not work late at night, get up too early and start working again, go to school, and push yourself all day. Who can be a great teacher if he or she is continually weary? Do not give a test to every student on Friday and spend fifteen or twenty hours during the weekend grading the tests. Spread out the homework and tests throughout the week. Give the amount of work that best teaches the student. Fifty math problems are not needed to practice one math skill. The goal is to practice and to better learn the skill, not to learn it and then begin to hate it as you complete forty redundant problems after you mastered the skill in problems one to ten.

Work hard and work smart. Do not cut corners, do not hand out worksheet after worksheet, do not give busywork assignments. Create classroom activities and homework projects that fascinate the students. Piling on the worksheets turns off the brains of students and then they misbehave, giving you stacks of worksheets to grade and misbehavior to correct.

Talk to the best teachers in the school to see how they balance their work, their time, their tests, their homework, planning lessons, grading papers, going to meetings, keeping up with computer work, and everything else.

Have a wholesome life outside of school: family, friends, exercise, volunteer work, a movie, church activities if you are involved in a church, a Saturday afternoon nap, and a Friday night free from all school-related work.

I'm eager to hear your questions, so let's take a quick break and then see what is on your mind. (Author's note: What questions would you expect? How can these new teachers get answers to their current and future questions by listening to teachers?)

CASE STUDY 8.3

The graduate school class in educational administration that Wesley Madison was taking had already created a dilemna that had personal, professional, ethical implications. Wesley had been a very respected high school math teacher for eight years. He had questioned his career choice very seriously when he completed his third year of teaching. At that time he was twenty-five years old, single, and certain that he could easily find another job that applied his 4.0 grade point average in college math classes.

He stayed in teaching because teaching stayed in him. Wesley could use his math knowledge in a variety of jobs, but teaching had always been his dream, his calling, his vision of himself, so he decided to continue.

By age thirty Wesley was married, the father of a two-year-old boy, and another child would be born in four months. Wesley's wife, Anne, was a nurse who worked two twelve-hour shifts on weekends. Wesley and Anne hoped she could reduce her part-time status to one twelve-hour shift after their second child was born. To help with the family finances, Wesley was completing a graduate school program to become certified as a school administrator. His certification would qualify him to apply for administration jobs as the principal or assistant principal of an elementary school, middle school, or high school. Wesley strongly hoped to stay at the high school level to build on his experience and achievements there.

Administrative work would mean more time away from home, from family. Administrative work would mean a larger income. Administrative work would take Wesley out of the high school math classroom and into the school office. These were agonizing trade-offs, but for his family's finances, the job change was essential. He promised himself to make time for family and not let an administrative job have any negative impact on his life at home.

Wesley completed his graduate school program and earned his administrative certification in May, about the same time that the school year ended in his school district. On a very exciting day in mid-June, Wesley took Anne to the hospital, and eight hours later their daughter was born. In July, Wesley interviewed for an assistant principal job at a middle school and an assistant principal job at a high school, but not the high school where he had taught.

The high school principal of the school where Wesley interviewed e-mailed him to say, "Thank you for interviewing with us. Our interview committee and I have decided to go in another direction. We wish you well in your career." Wesley was disappointed but not distressed. He concluded that anyone who e-mails a rejection notice and who hides behind the superficial code of "decided to go in another direction" was not the best person for him to work for.

The middle school principal called Wesley and asked if he could come to the school. The principal said that some meetings just needed to be face-to-face, but he did tell Wesley that he would recommend him for the assistant principal job and with agreement from the school district superintendent and school board it would be official.

The meeting with the middle school principal was inspiring. "Our interviewing committee and I are very impressed with your experience and with your credentials. We would be delighted to have you work here as our assistant principal. As you know, middle school is quite different from high school and administration is very different from teaching." As he heard those words, time froze as Wesley's thoughts raced. This would be a significant career step for Wesley and could create further opportunities as a school principal, then a central office administrator, possibly a school district superintendent much later in his career.

Wesley had interviewed very sincerely, and he knew that moving into an administration job was the right decision, yet could not avoid dozens of questions that almost haunted him at this moment. Will he miss the classroom? Will he ever get to interact with students in the wonderful ways he did as a teacher? Will administration work change him, and will he like the change? If he does not become an administrator now when will he get another chance? Will the extra money be worth the extra hours at school to supervise events in the evening, to attend meetings after school dismisses, to deal with some of the extremely disagreeable parents or guardians, to deal with students who create situations that violate rules and violate laws?

Those thoughts flew through Wesley's mind simultaneously so there was no real pause in the conversation. Wesley replied as he had already decided he would reply, "Thank you, sir. I would be honored to be the assistant principal of this school."

The conversation continued with topics that ranged from the paperwork involved with this job change to the specific administrative duties that Wesley would have. Wesley knew he had made the right decision for his family and for his career, but, well, after putting his heart into the classroom for eight years, it was an unexpected combination of excitement and apprehension, hope and anxiety, anticipation and reluctance, looking forward to a new job while thinking fond memories from the past eight years.

While driving home, Wesley made a promise to himself. What I do will change as I become an administrator. How I do my administrative work does not have to change. I can and I will take the heart, mind, and soul of a teacher with me to the job of assistant principal. That probably is idealistic, but it will be a hope that sustains me. I will do everything possible to be an assistant principal who always remembers that school is about students and that teachers know the students better than anyone else at school does.

Will Wesley Madison's plan work? Will he remember to listen to teachers? Will the day he has to testify in court about a student against whom charges were filed for an assault at school cause Wesley to lose his idealism? Can he do the required office work that administrators must do and still spend the time in the classroom that administrators know they should? If Wesley moves up the administrative ranks in his career and eventually works at a school district central office, what will he do to remain an educator and not let the bureaucracy make him a stereotypical bureaucrat?

Wesley could remember words of wisdom from a graduate school class about school administration. "Education cannot thrive one-half instructional and one-half bureaucratic. All educators must maximize the instructional and minimize the bureaucratic. Let teachers teach. Screen, question, evaluate every decision, action, policy, or procedure through the classroom impact filter. Does the currently proposed reform, law, policy, regulation, decision enhance, support, encourage the teaching and learning tasks in the classroom, or does the current proposal complicate, frustrate, and bureaucratize the teaching and learning tasks?"

CASE STUDY 8.4

Whereas the elected officials of the community of Walden have endured increasing federal government involvement in schools in direct violation of the Tenth Amendment of the United States Constitution;

Whereas the elected officials of the community of Walden have endured increasingly impossible requirements from state officials—all students will be physically fit students, all students will avoid bullying, all students will be vaccinated, all students whose families will not or cannot or just prefer to have someone else do it will be fed twice daily at school, all students will reach an ambitious academic standard yet the system of how scores showing achievement of that standard are calculated has been changed often and is being changed again—in direct violation of any realistic awareness of facts;

Whereas federal officials, state officials, social reformers, editorial writers, bureaucrats, television or radio program hosts, politicians, and advocacy group spokespeople could not do the job of a teacher, but insist on telling teachers what to accomplish, be it resolved now that

1. All students are declared to be smart.
2. All students are declared to be healthy.
3. All students are declared to be well behaved.

Since political and community leaders seem to think that passing a law or issuing a statement can improve education, we endorse this resolution and conclude that since we put it in writing and voted in favor of it, it must be true and by merely saying it is true, we conclude that we have made it true.

We should have thought of this years ago. It's much easier to say that something has been, should be, or will be done than it is to actually do something.

That fictional resolution raises a question about the ideal goals of a society's educational system and the current reality within that society and within its schools. People who work through legislation, laws, policies, regulations, political procedures, bureaucracies, elections, interest group efforts, or the media may have the most honorable of intentions about improving school. From those intentions to actual classroom implementation of instruction that causes the intended learning can be a wide, massive divide. Listening to teachers is an essential part of bridging that divide and, consequently, of moving the classroom reality closer to the societal goal.

Teaching well is very hard work. Teaching well in a classroom today is harder work than teaching has ever been. Educating students well is more important now than ever before. What is to be done so the hard work of teaching results in the expected academic achievement of students?

One part of the answer to that question is listen to teachers, the people who most accurately know the classroom. Among the aspects of school that teachers uniquely know is the classroom reality—what works, what does not work, what helps, what does not help, what is needed, what is not needed, how students are doing, and how students need to be doing.

Among the fascinating and vital lessons I learned when, after being a school administrator for thirteen years, I taught high school again is that people who seek to improve schools must listen to teachers. Progress begins with a full and accurate understanding of the current reality. School progress begins with a full and accurate understanding of what only teachers can explain about the current classroom reality.

EPILOGUE
Be Like Murphy

In the eighth year of my thirteen-year adventure as a middle school assistant principal, I was asked by Jim Thomas, the principal of the school, if I would like to teach a class. What a bold, powerful, brilliant idea. Jim Thomas's leadership skills are exemplary. He knew the students would learn from me. He knew that teachers and I would have a new connection as I lived part of each day doing the work that fills their days. He knew how encouraging the experience would be for me.

During most of those six years when I taught one class, the subject was economics. The last year I worked at that school was the year I taught an economics class that Murphy Jones took. He mastered the class brilliantly. His creative insights, ideas, and projects were uniquely Murphy. It was a joy to be his teacher.

The high school classroom called me, and I answered the call. As life worked out these matters, I became a teacher at the high school where Murphy was becoming a ninth grader. I taught eleventh graders, but I saw Murphy at school very often. He loved high school. He told me about his classes, about the school's soccer team he played for, about how neat it was to be out of middle school and into high school.

This book is dedicated to Murphy Jones, a student who was liked by everyone, who was loved by many people, and who is missed beyond

EPILOGUE

what words can communicate. I hope that I will get to be a teacher in heaven. I hope that Murphy Jones will be in my first heavenly class.

I am very thankful that I had the opportunities to listen to Murphy's amazing ideas in class and to listen to his vibrant reports about high school. One reminder I take from that is to listen to students. As a teacher who works from the premise that students are real people living real lives right now, listening to students is as important to teachers as listening to teachers is for people who seek to improve education.

In the closing pages the reader will get to listen to part of the story of Murphy Jones. After reading those pages, please go listen extra closely to your students.

BE LIKE MURPHY

I have been a teacher or a school administrator for twenty-three years. The most difficult day during those twenty-three years was Friday, February 9, 2007. On that day I arrived very early at the high school where I was a U.S. history teacher. First-period class begins at 8:30 a.m., but I arrived at 6:57 a.m. to prepare an extra study guide for my advanced placement scholars. Recent snowstorms had closed school for a few days, and those classes had to work at a faster pace, so I had to give the students the tools to make that pace possible.

At 8:40 a.m. an assistant principal came to the classroom door and knocked. I would give all I own if the conversation that followed had not been necessary.

"Could I talk to you for a minute?" he asked in a straightforward, proper way. I have been an assistant principal so I have gone to classrooms with the same request. I replied, "Yes, sir."

He asked, "You know Murphy Jones, don't you?"

"Sure. I taught him in eighth grade. I see him a lot at this high school. I was just talking to him a few days ago." I thought that the administrator might need my help to provide some information. Murphy did great work in my economics class. We have had many wonderful conversations through the years about our favorite sport—soccer. So I was ready to help the assistant principal and Murphy in whatever was needed. I was not ready for the next statement.

"Murphy died. We just got a call. We knew you had taught him, so we wanted you to hear this in person."

Now what? My students expect me to return for the rest of our discussion of World War I; however, there is a world war being fought in my heart, mind, body, and soul. This news of Murphy, a fifteen-year-old friend of mine just cannot be true, but it is true. Sometimes life hurts. At that moment life was causing hurt that defies description.

My only choice was to teach through the pain. My brain bounced between President Woodrow Wilson's hope that the Great War would make the world safe for all humanity and my hope that life could be safe for fifteen-year-olds.

I taught my five classes with the vigor and confidence of an actor who knows that the show must go on. I taught with a clear and certain voice that hid my clouded and uncertain thoughts. I taught with a broken heart, but with the hope that through teaching well I could touch the lives of teenagers who, like Murphy did, should live vibrantly.

I would be a better person if I were more like Murphy. Murphy had many, many friends whom he made time for. Murphy had a ready smile. Murphy was conscientious about school, fascinated with soccer, and eager to achieve. Murphy was polite, friendly, and disciplined. He was active at school, in his church, in the community, in Boy Scouts.

After school on February 9, 2007, I went to the tennis club where I exercised. I talked to some teenagers whom I know from school. I added some extra words of encouragement to them because tomorrow is promised to no one. I must make each moment count more and better.

When I got in my car to drive home the tears flowed. Tears that were told at 8:40 a.m. to wait now insisted on waiting no longer. I rarely cry. I've cried more about Murphy's death than I have cried in the past five years.

I cherish the memory of my last conversation with Murphy. He said school was going well. We talked about soccer. I introduced him to another teacher. As we parted, Murphy broadly smiled. I will see that smile forever. I will seek to match that smile of Murphy's with a more frequent smile of my own. I will seek to be like Murphy.

As I write these words, I cry, yet I also smile a little in joyous appreciation of knowing Murphy. Thanks, Murphy, you taught me well. You are still teaching me well. How I wish I could still teach you. Let's take a class together in heaven and then play an eternal game of soccer.

ABOUT THE AUTHOR

Keen Babbage has been involved in education for twenty-four years as a teacher and administrator at the middle school and high school levels. He has also taught graduate school classes and has written eight other books about education. He currently teaches U.S. history and political science at Henry Clay High School in Lexington, Kentucky.